Oliver Optic

Bivouac and Battle

Or, The Struggles of a Soldier

Oliver Optic

Bivouac and Battle
Or, The Struggles of a Soldier

ISBN/EAN: 9783337136048

Printed in Europe, USA, Canada, Australia, Japan

Cover: Foto ©ninafisch / pixelio.de

More available books at **www.hansebooks.com**

The Gentleman who sat opposite. Page 43.

THE UPWARD AND ONWARD SERIES.

BIVOUAC AND BATTLE;

OR, THE

STRUGGLES OF A SOLDIER.

BY

OLIVER OPTIC,

AUTHOR OF "YOUNG AMERICA ABROAD," "THE ARMY AND NAVY STORIES," "THE WOODVILLE STORIES," "THE BOAT-CLUB STORIES," "THE STARRY FLAG SERIES," "THE LAKE-SHORE SERIES," ETC.

WITH FOURTEEN ILLUSTRATIONS.

BOSTON:
LEE AND SHEPARD, PUBLISHERS.
NEW YORK:
LEE, SHEPARD AND DILLINGHAM.
1873.

TO

MY YOUNG FRIEND

FRANK C. FOSTER,
OF CANANDAIGUA, N. Y.,

𝔗𝔥𝔦𝔰 𝔅𝔬𝔬𝔨

IS AFFECTIONATELY DEDICATED.

THE UPWARD AND ONWARD SERIES.

1. *Field and Forest;* or, The Fortunes of a Farmer.

2. *Plane and Plank;* or, The Mishaps of a Mechanic.

3. *Desk and Debit;* or, The Catastrophes of a Clerk.

4. *Cringle and Cross-Tree;* or, The Sea Swashes of a Sailor.

5. *Bivouac and Battle;* or, The Struggles of a Soldier.

IN PREPARATION.

6. *Sea and Shore;* or, The Tramps of a Traveller.

PREFACE.

"BIVOUAC AND BATTLE" is the fifth of the ONWARD AND UPWARD SERIES, in which Phil Farringford appears as a soldier. The events of the story are located in New York, on the Atlantic, in England, and at the seat of war in Italy in 1859. The hero continues to be a Christian young man, who labors to make his life an upward and onward progress, even while his adventures are stirring and exciting; though perhaps it is more difficult to be honest, upright, and noble in the dull monotony of an uneventful career than in one filled with changing incidents, and checkered with life's vicissitudes. Whatever happens to Phil, he is always true to himself, true to his friends, and true to his God.

Larry Grimsby appears at first as a reckless young man, addicted to the vices which are unhappily so often embraced by the young, especially in large cities. Phil obtains an influence over him, by the events of the story, which proves to be beneficial to his friend. The episode of Mr. Fennimore, the bank officer, contains the history of too many, in the present generation, who are tempted to do wrong in the beginning, with the intention of making restitution at a future time, but are carried away into the vortex of crime, from which they find it impossible to escape.

The reader will doubtless sympathize with Phil Farringford in the happiness of seeing his family united under one roof, in peace, joy, and prosperity; and it is hoped that he will not fail to observe that this result is achieved by the practice of Christian principles, which saved his father from intemperance, and enabled him to bring his parents together.

HARRISON SQUARE, BOSTON,
          November 25, 1871.

CONTENTS.

CHAPTER I.
PAGE
IN WHICH PHIL FARRINGFORD FALLS IN WITH LARRY GRIMSBY. 11

CHAPTER II.
IN WHICH PHIL LEARNS MORE ABOUT LARRY GRIMSBY, AND THE TRAIN ARRIVES AT NEW YORK. 24

CHAPTER III.
IN WHICH PHIL COMPLETES HIS PREPARATIONS FOR THE VOYAGE, AND GOES ON BOARD THE STEAMER. . . . 38

CHAPTER IV.
IN WHICH PHIL WALKS ABOUT THE DECK, AND FINDS ANOTHER GRIMSBY. 51

CHAPTER V.
IN WHICH PHIL LISTENS TO THE DEFAULTER'S STORY, AND BECOMES BETTER ACQUAINTED WITH BLANCHE FENNIMORE. 65

CHAPTER VI.
IN WHICH PHIL HAS A MELANCHOLY PASSAGE ACROSS THE ATLANTIC. 80

CHAPTER VII.
IN WHICH PHIL AND HIS FRIEND VISIT GRIMSBY HALL, AND ARE PRESENT AT A MELANCHOLY OCCASION. . . 94

CHAPTER VIII.
IN WHICH PHIL SHOWS THAT HE HAS A TALENT FOR KEEPING STILL, AND LARRY BECOMES A HERO. 108

CHAPTER IX.
IN WHICH PHIL RELATES THE STORY THE BARONET TOLD, AND LARRY MEETS BLANCHE IN THE GARDEN. . . . 122

CHAPTER X.
IN WHICH PHIL AND LARRY GO TO LONDON, AND MILES GRIMSBY IS VERY MUCH EXCITED. 136

CHAPTER XI.
IN WHICH PHIL AND LARRY MAKE THE ACQUAINTANCE OF A MAN WITH A PREPOSTEROUS HAT, AND START FOR ITALY. 150

CHAPTER XII.
IN WHICH PHIL AND LARRY CONTINUE THEIR JOURNEY, AND MEET A FRENCH GENERAL OF BRIGADE. 163

CHAPTER XIII.
IN WHICH PHIL AND LARRY BECOME SOLDIERS, AND SPEND THEIR FIRST NIGHT IN BIVOUAC. 177

CHAPTER XIV.
IN WHICH PHIL AND LARRY MOVE FORWARD WITH THE ARMY, AND DECIDE TO VISIT MILAN. 191

CHAPTER XV.
IN WHICH PHIL AND LARRY FLOAT DOWN THE CANAL, AND ARE DISTURBED BY FRENCH PICKET GUARDS. 205

CHAPTER XVI.
IN WHICH PHIL AND LARRY DISCUSS THE SITUATION, AND FACE A DRUM-HEAD COURT-MARTIAL. 219

CHAPTER XVII.
In which Phil and Larry are saved from a hard Fate by a Movement of the Brigade. 233

CHAPTER XVIII.
In which Phil and Larry solve a Problem, and the Italian makes a bad Move. 246

CHAPTER XIX.
In which Phil invents and launches an Aquatic Machine, and prepares to cross the Ticino. 260

CHAPTER XX.
In which Phil and Larry take Part in the Battle of Magenta, and visit Milan. 273

CHAPTER XXI.
In which Phil is identified by his Mother, and Larry goes to England. 286

CHAPTER XXII.
In which Phil remonstrates with Larry, who decides to go up in a Balloon. 300

CHAPTER XXIII.
In which Phil is very anxious about Larry, who has a perilous Adventure in the Balloon. . . . 314

CHAPTER XXIV.
In which Phil and Larry visit Grimsby Hall, and return to America. 327

BIVOUAC AND BATTLE;

OR,

THE STRUGGLES OF A SOLDIER.

CHAPTER I.

IN WHICH PHIL FARRINGFORD FALLS IN WITH LARRY GRIMSBY.

"HELP! Help!"

I uttered these impressive words myself, for I felt that my lamp of life was on the point of being extinguished. I had struggled till my strength was exhausted, and I had lost all hope of being able to extricate myself from the perilous situation in which I was placed.

Unfortunately, railroad accidents are too common in the United States to need a detailed description. I was on my way from St. Louis to New York, intending to embark in a steamer for Europe. I was tired of the monotony of the railroad train, and only anxious to reach my destina-

tion. It was the last day of the long journey,—
longer then than now,—and late in the evening I
expected to be in the great city; but our best laid
calculations often end in defeat and disaster. I
had bought a book of the boy who frequently
passed through the train with a bundle of literary
merchandise. The work was David Copperfield,
and I was following with intense interest the fortunes of the hero, when suddenly I heard a crash-
ing sound under us, as the cars were crossing a
bridge. The structure had given way, and the
carriage dropped down into the stream.

In another instant the passengers were struggling in the water, which, in the part where I was,
rose nearly to the ceiling thereof. I had so often
confronted danger and disaster, that I did not
regard the situation as at all desperate. I stood
on the seat, and thus elevated my head above the
water. I had been sitting by a window. It was
one of the earliest days in May, and the weather
was remarkably warm. During the hour preceding
the disaster, I had raised the sash a dozen times;
but the fastenings were out of order, and it would
persist in coming down with a smash as often as I
adjusted it. I had tried to wedge it up with a roll

of paper; but this experiment had failed, and I was so much interested in Copperfield, that I abandoned further attempts to supply myself with fresh air for the moment.

Stooping down from my standing position on the chair, I raised the window; but the upper part of the aperture was at least a foot under water. I heard people at work on the roof with axes, cutting a hole through which the passengers might make their escape; but I was afraid the service would be rendered too late for some of them. My end of the car was sunk deeper than the other in the water; but the passengers were crowded together in that part, and the door there seemed to be obstructed by the debris of the shattered carriages in the rear. My impulse, therefore, was to effect my exit from the dangerous situation by the window nearest to me.

Having lifted the sash, the way seemed to be clear and practicable, as I was a strong and skilful swimmer, and was almost as much at home in the water as on the land. But that window, which had vexed me so much while I was reading, was destined to give me more serious trouble than before. Holding the sash with my hand, I dropped my head quickly under the surface of the water, thrust it through the open window, and crowded my body after it. Of course, in doing this I was obliged to release my hold of the sash. Springing for the surface of the water outside of the car, I believed my individual trials nearly at an end. Unluckily, the sash was loose enough to fall by its own weight even in the water, and in spite of the swelling of the wood-work, which it must have caused. It dropped upon my legs, and shut down tightly upon my ankles in such a way that I found it quite impossible to release them from its grip.

In vain I twisted my body, squirmed, and struggled. The sash seemed to be wedged immovably upon my legs. The end of the car also appeared to be sinking deeper in the water, and with my utmost efforts I could only occasionally get my head to the surface of the river for a breath of air. I felt that my last moment on earth had come, and having shouted for help, I commended my soul to God, and prayed for my father and mother, that they might be reunited, in a single phrase. The men who were cutting the hole in the top of the car did not seem to see me; but after I had cried for assistance, I was conscious that some one came to the edge of the roof, near me. I struggled again.

"What's the matter?" was the question that hardly penetrated my semi-conscious brain.

I could make no reply; I could only gasp, as I succeeded for an instant in getting my mouth to the surface again.

"Help! Help!"

My friend on the top dropped into the water. I felt his hand upon my legs, but it was still some time before he succeeded in releasing me, for he was obliged to operate under the surface of the stream. He worked my deliverance at last, and I rose into the free air of heaven. My strength was all gone; I had not even enough left to climb to the roof of the carriage; and I should certainly have sunk and perished if my deliverer had not grasped me with his strong arm, and dragged me upon the top of the car. The end which had been the scene of my struggles was now partially submerged; but I sat down near the verge of the water, to recover my exhausted energies.

By this time the axe-men had made a hole large enough to permit the passage of the unfortunate passengers beneath me. My strength came back to me in a few moments, and I walked to the shore. I had the consolation of seeing and knowing, that if I had remained in the car, as my companions had done, I should have been saved without a struggle for myself. Happily, in this instance not a single passenger was killed, though several were more or less injured. A poor brakeman was instantly deprived of life by being crushed in the falling train. As soon as I recovered my powers of mind and body, I began to look about me with interest for the brave and unselfish fellow who had saved my life. He had accomplished it at no little peril and effort, and my gratitude for my preservation was unbounded. I thanked God with all my heart for his goodness to me, for I felt that I owed my safety first to him, and next to my gallant friend. I discovered him still busy in his wet garments, rendering assistance to the injured and terrified passengers. As I was now completely restored, I felt able to do something myself. I worked for half an hour, till we had done everything within our means for the comfort of the injured.

The forward part of the train, including the

LARRY GRIMSBY GIVES PHIL A LIFT. Page 15.

baggage and two passenger cars, had crossed the bridge in safety, while two more had fallen through the broken timbers. One of these was almost a total wreck, and was now half under water, while the other rested half on the bridge and half in the stream.

I went to the baggage car, and found my trunk, from which I took a change of clothing, and put it on in the smoking-car saloon. The conductor had sent the engine and tender forward to the next considerable station for assistance, and in due time it returned with a large gang of men and several cars. Another train was soon made up after its arrival, and in three hours from the accident we were again on our way to New York. As soon as the cars started, I sought again for my deliverer, whose labors were now ended. I did not find him at first, but I walked through the train till I discovered him, seated alone in front of one who had been injured by the calamity, whom he seemed to have in charge.

"My friend, I owe you a debt of gratitude which I shall never be able to discharge," I began.

"You? 'Pon my word, I don't know that I

ever saw you before in my life," replied he, opening his eyes, and looking at me all over.

"Indeed! Don't you remember that you rescued me at the car window, when I was completely used up?"

"O, are you the individual? No, you are not; he was dressed in light clothes."

"But I was wet and uncomfortable, and I changed my dress."

"That's it! Well, you look like the fellow I helped out. By the way, that was an odd kind of a scrape you got into."

"It was, indeed; and without your help, I should not have been among the living at this moment."

"So?" said he, with a smile.

"I speak only the literal truth. I assure you my heart is full of gratitude to you for your noble efforts in my behalf."

"O, never mind that. A fellow can't help doing what he can for one that needs his assistance in such a scrape as that. This is the third time in five years I have been smashed on a railroad train, and never had a hair of my head damaged. 'Pon my word, I'm getting used to such things, and if

I have many more, I shall learn to enjoy the excitement of them. Going to New York?"

"Yes, sir."

"So am I."

"Then I hope I shall see more of you, and be able to express my gratitude to you, at least, if I am not permitted to do anything more."

"Never mind that, Mr. Jones; don't say another word about it. I hate gratitude; and if you had saved my life, I don't believe I should feel a bit of gratitude."

"However you may feel, I am certainly very grateful to you, and I shall never forget, or cease to appreciate, your service to me."

"Don't do it, Mr. Jones. As a special favor to me, forget all about it, and cease at once to appreciate, and all that sort of thing."

"I cannot be so heartless, my friend."

"Try, Mr. Jones; try. I hate to place any one under obligations to me."

"I certainly will not burden you with the expression of my gratitude, since it is offensive to you; but I cannot help feeling it."

"All right, Mr. Jones; I don't care what you feel, if you don't compel me to feel it, too," laughed he. "You seem to be a good fellow, Mr. Jones."

"My name is Farringford."

"Excuse me, Mr. Farringford, for I have a habit of calling everybody Jones when I don't know his name. I'm not a Yankee; but I have a habit of asking questions. I dare say Farringford is not all your name."

"Not quite. My first name is Philip; but my intimate friends usually call me Phil."

"That's a capital name; and as I claim to be your intimate friend, I shall take the liberty to call you Phil, for I can't afford to utter anybody's name when it consists of three syllables. I can get off two very well, but I always break down on three. My name is Lawrence Grimsby, but everybody that knows me calls me Larry; and you will oblige me by adopting the custom of my intimates. Larry, at your service. What's this?" asked he, as the train began to break up.

It was an important station, and our car stopped directly before the refreshment saloon. Larry rose in his seat, and looked out at the window.

"That's a refreshment saloon," said he.

"Yes; there is the sign."

"Phil, you're evidently a good fellow," he added, looking at me, though I could perceive a peculiar embarrassment in his manner.

"I try to do my duty to myself and my friends," I replied.

"I thought so. I shall do you the honor to let you pay for a light lunch for me. I'm hungry, and I'm dead broke — two things as consistent with each other as they are annoying and uncomfortable to me."

"Certainly, my dear Larry —"

"Hold on, Phil! Don't you go to dearing me; I won't stand it; and if you do so, 'pon my word I won't let you disburse a red cent for me."

"Come along, Larry. You shall have your own will in everything," I answered, leading the way out of the car, and into the refreshment saloon.

His humor was so peculiar that I dared not say anything more to give vent to my feelings. I was absolutely shocked when he said he was hungry, and had no money. My heart swelled with emotion, and even my eyes were disposed to shed a few tears; for it was really horrible to think of my deliverer being actually hungry. I would have given him my purse at once, and I was burning to pour out my gratitude in words, but I dared not do either. It was the middle of the afternoon, and I had dined about two o'clock, so that I was not hungry myself. Probably for the want of funds he had not dined at all, or he could not have been in his present condition in a couple of hours. He ate oysters, hard-boiled eggs, cold ham, pies and cakes, like one who had not tasted food for twenty-four hours.

"Don't be alarmed, Phil," said he, as he continued his meal with unabated relish.

"I am not alarmed," I replied, as I took a piece of cake, rather for the sociability of eating with him than because I wanted it. "Help yourself, and be entirely at home."

"I hope your funds are in good condition, Phil," laughed he.

"In very good condition, indeed."

"I'm an odd stick, Phil, and don't eat every day in the week."

"You don't!"

"Of course not. It would be a waste of time; but when I do eat, I make a business of it, for I may not think it worth while to do this thing again for a day or two."

"Why not?"

"Because it doesn't pay to keep eating all the time. Your jolly old philosopher, Dr. Franklin, got up a calculation of the vast quantity of grub that a useless fellow consumes; but he didn't figure up the time that is wasted in dining-rooms and refreshment saloons."

"I don't think the people of this country waste any time at their meals."

"A very just observation, Phil. Possibly, if I always found a dollar in my pocket when I put my hand into it, I might alter my views," added Larry, with a sickly smile, as the bell rang for the train to start. "That means you and me. I've eaten all I want. Humph! I may not do it again for a week."

I paid the bill, which amounted to one dollar and forty cents, with a pleasure I cannot express, and we took our seats in the train again.

CHAPTER II.

IN WHICH PHIL LEARNS MORE ABOUT LARRY GRIMSBY, AND THE TRAIN ARRIVES AT NEW YORK.

I HAVE introduced the railroad accident, which is too common an event to be a novelty, in order solely to present Larry Grimsby to my friends. I am sure, if I had met him under any other circumstances, I should not have thought of making his acquaintance. He was a young man of eighteen or nineteen, which was about my own age. Physically he was well formed, and his face was rather a good-looking one; but here, to a casual observer of my own tastes and habits, his attractions would have ceased. He was well dressed, but his appearance was rather flashy. His pants were of light material, with an enormous plaid upon them. His vest was marked with an absurd perpendicular stripe, and his coat was of light green, cut in the jauntiest style of the time.

Although, under other circumstances, he was not a person whose acquaintance I should have sought, I realized that he was a noble fellow at heart. If there had been no railroad accident, I might have despised him as long as I remembered him, for the "cut of his jib" prejudiced me against him. For a young man, he was a very eccentric one. While he objected to any expression of gratitude on my part, he did not hesitate to ask me to pay for his lunch. Independent of the priceless service he had rendered me, I confess that I felt a deep interest in him. He acknowledged that he had not even money enough to pay for his dinner, and, after his fashion, had declared that he did not expect to have another meal for a day or two. I looked at him, and tried to make up my mind what he was; but he was a problem to me, and I could not fathom him.

"I feel better, Phil," said he, as we resumed our seats in the car.

"I should think you would, if you had not been to dinner," I replied, hoping to draw him out.

"I certainly had not been to dinner, and hardly to breakfast. I haven't even one cent of money, or anything that I can turn into money. I sold my watch in Buffalo to obtain the means to pay my fare to New York."

"But you have friends?"

"Certainly I have; and you are one of them."

"I mean relatives."

"Humph! Not that I am aware of," he replied, lightly.

"Where do you belong?"

"I belong here."

"You have a home somewhere, I mean."

"A home!" exclaimed he, with a laugh. "What's that?"

"Of course you know what a home is."

"Can't say I do, Phil."

"Did you never have a home?"

"Never a home; of late years, at least."

"Have you no father and mother?" I asked, my interest in the young man increasing every moment.

"Never saw or heard of any such individuals."

"My dear fellow —"

"Hold on, Phil; I don't want any one sympathizing with me. I don't need it. I never had any father or mother, so far as I know, nor a relative, nor any other person who cared a fig for me, and I don't know but I have been the gainer by it."

"I think not," I replied, shaking my head.

"Perhaps you know better than I."

"It is reasonable that a young man should be the better for a mother's influence and a father's care. One's parents usually teach him the ways of morality and truth, give him his religious impressions — "

"I don't believe in any of those things, and don't trouble my head at all about them."

"You shock me."

"Do I?" laughed he.

"You do, indeed. Don't you believe in religion?"

"I believe there is such a thing, but it don't trouble me, and I don't trouble religion. I do about what is right when it is convenient."

"I am sure you would think more of religion, and that you would desire to do what is right, even when it is not wholly convenient, if you had had a good mother to teach you the way of life and truth."

"Don't preach, Phil; it's worse than gratitude and sympathy. I'm not a perfect young man, I know."

"Where were you born, Larry?"

"I don't know; I haven't the least idea."

"But you had a beginning somewhere."

"I was a graduate from an orphan asylum when I was eight years old. An old lady saw me there, and thought I was a pretty boy; so she took me home with her. She gave me a very good education, and I staid with her till I was fourteen years old. She always used me well, and taught me piety, catechism, and religion, which I got rid of as soon as possible. I supposed the old lady, who had plenty of money, would leave me her fortune; but she didn't do it; and since that I have been a sceptic on the subject of gratitude. I had allowed her to spend her money on me, in feeding, clothing, and educating me, and then she was so cruel as to die without making a will in my favor, or of anybody else, for that matter. As soon as the breath had left her body, about a dozen and a half of nephews and nieces stepped in, and in due time her money was equally divided among them. Not a penny gladdened the interior of my purse."

"Perhaps she intended to do something for you."

"I think she did; and the ingratitude was in

the neglect to do it. She died suddenly, and never knew a thing after she was taken sick, so that my wheels were blocked. Not one of the nieces and nephews even looked at me; and when the old lady's house was sold, I was turned out into the street. Since then I have been a wanderer on the face of the footstool."

"But what did you do with yourself?" I asked.

"I found a place to work in a store; but I didn't like it, and then I learned the printing business. I work as a jour printer now, when I work at all. I have been cruising about the west for the last year. I work a while in one place, and then move on to another. I subbed a while in Buffalo, and then got cut of a job, and had to sell my watch, as I said, to enable me to get to New York."

"Don't you know anything about your parents?"

"Not a thing; and I haven't the least idea how I happened to be in the orphan asylum. To tell the truth, Phil, I don't care a fig, either. If my parents didn't want me, I'm sure I don't want them. If I could know who they were for the asking, I wouldn't open my mouth. That's so, Phil."

"You are a strange being, Larry."

"I know it; and I would just as lief live as die."

"So would I."

"Well, put it the other way; I had just as lief die as live. I don't know that I care a straw for anything in this world — or any other, for that matter," laughed he. "Who are you, Phil?"

I answered this blunt inquiry, though it required a couple of hours to satisfy his curiosity, for he questioned me very closely. I told him that I had been brought up in a cabin on the Upper Missouri, where I had only a rough backwoodsman for a companion for several years; that I had found my father in St. Louis, who had separated from my mother, and that I intended to visit Europe in order to find her if possible. He drew out of me all the particulars of my eventful history.

"Then you are as rich as mud, Phil."

"Not very rich."

"I figure up that you have three or four thousand dollars in your own right."

"That isn't much."

"I'm nineteen, but I never had fifty dollars in my life at one time."

"I suppose you are not careful of your money."

"I'm careful to spend it as soon as I get it. That's what money is for."

" But you can't have it and spend it too."

" I'm not a miser."

" Nor I, any more than you. I spend money for what I need, and save the rest. In that way I gathered my little pile."

I took out my purse, which contained twenty-two half eagles; for at the time of which I write there was no national currency, that was good in all the states, and I had changed my money into gold before I left the west, for the bank bills of one section of the country were subject to a discount in other sections. I turned the coins out into my hand, and Larry watched me with interest. Taking twenty of the half eagles, or one hundred dollars, I handed them to him.

" Put them in your pocket," I added.

" What do you mean?" asked he, taking the money into his hand.

" Put them in your pocket," I repeated. " Possibly, when you get to New York, you will find time to eat a dinner or two; and you will need some of this coin to pay the bill."

" Do I understand you to say that you make me a present of these shiners?"

"Precisely so; that's just what I mean, if you will allow me to state it in that offensive manner."

"I thank you with all my heart," said he, but without much emotion. "I never was so rich before in my life. You do not state on what grounds you do this magnificent thing."

"Simply because you are a good fellow, Larry," I replied, mindful of his instruction in regard to gratitude.

"That is all-sufficient ground. By the way, Phil, I helped a dozen people after the accident, and you are the only one who has offered me a cent for my trouble."

"Why, you would not have them attempt to pay you for such service."

"Certainly not."

"I dare say they are all very grateful to you for what you did."

"I don't believe they are; and I hope they are not. Never mind them. The railroad accident was the luckiest thing that has happened for me in the whole course of my life," continued Larry, as he chinked the coins in his hand, and then put them in his pocket. "To what hotel do you go in New York, Phil?"

"I thought I should go to the Western Hotel."

"That's not first-class."

"The prices are not first-class, either," I added.

"But you have plenty of money, unless you have robbed yourself to enrich a good fellow."

"I have ten or a dozen dollars left," I replied.

"But I will give you back half or all you gave me, if you have made yourself short."

"No, no; I have a draft for over two thousand dollars to pay my expenses in Europe. Don't trouble yourself about the little matter I gave you."

"I won't," said he, laughing. "But I thought I should go to the St. Nicholas Hotel, now that I have my pile."

"You will have to pay two or three dollars a day."

"What of it, when a fellow has a hundred dollars in hard shiners in his trousers pocket?"

"You won't have them, or any of them, long, if you do business in that way, Larry. What hotel were you going to if you had not met me?"

"To none; I should have gone to a cheap boarding-house, and then looked out for a job in a printing office. But I won't be odd, Phil. If you are going to the Western Hotel, I will go with you, though it isn't first-class."

"I dare say it is quite as good as your cheap boarding-house would have been," I replied.

"No doubt of that; but circumstances alter cases, and even change printers' cases sometimes."

"I hope you will be able to find a place to work when you get to New York."

"Humph! I don't know," he answered, measuring off the words very slowly. "I shall not look for any place."

"Not look for any!" I exclaimed.

"No, I think not."

"Why not?"

"I have plenty of money in my pocket now," laughed he. "When it is gone, it will be time enough to go to work."

"That's very bad philosophy," I protested, emphatically.

"O, dear, Phil, I'm no philosopher. It would be quite impossible for me to go to work with even five dollars in my pocket."

"Then you are a regular vagabond, Larry."

"Phil, give me your hand!" exclaimed he,

grasping mine. "You have hit the nail on the head, exactly. I am a regular vagabond."

"But I wonld not be a vagabond, nor allow any one to call me by such a name."

"I always speak the truth myself when it is convenient; and I never object when anybody else does so. Here's a station, Phil, and the train is stopping. Let's get out, and stretch our legs."

We left the car. It was a large town, and the train stopped at the side of a street, on which there were hotels, saloons, and stores of various kinds.

"Here we are, Phil. That's just what I was looking for."

"What?"

"A bar-room. I was going to ask you to pay for a glass of brandy for me; but — "

"It would have been of no use to ask me, for no amount of gratitude, or anything else, could have induced me to do such a thing."

"Is that so?"

"That's so; most emphatically, decidedly, and unalterably so."

"You interrupted what I was saying. You

have put me in funds, and I was going to treat. Come along, Phil. You can take a glass of wine, if brandy don't agree with your constitution."

" Not a drop of anything for me."

" You are not going to make me drink alone — are you? "

" Alone if at all, so far as I am concerned," I replied.

" Take lemonade then, or some other slops."

" I will not even enter a bar-room."

" 'Pon my word, Phil, I didn't think so good a fellow as you are could be a fanatic."

" I am a fanatic on that subject, and I mean to be one to the end of my days."

" It's mean to drink alone."

" Don't do it then. We will take a cup of coffee, if you like."

" All right; coffee it is, Phil."

We drank coffee, and I paid for it. When we returned to the train, I laid down my principles in detail, illustrating them with the sad example of my father. Larry only laughed at me for my pains. I was sorry to find that the jaunty coat, the striped vest, and the plaid pants had not belied my new friend. I had the satisfaction of believing that the hundred dollars I had presented to him would be expended in a few days in extravagant living, drinks, and dissipation generally. I was sorry I had been so liberal; and while I was still very grateful to Larry, I was almost disgusted with him.

In the small hours of the morning, four hours behind time, the train arrived at New York, and we made our way to the Western Hotel.

CHAPTER III.

IN WHICH PHIL COMPLETES HIS PREPARATIONS FOR THE VOYAGE, AND GOES ON BOARD THE STEAMER.

I WAS grieved and mortified to find that my new friend was a young man of no principle, a vagabond, and, for aught I knew, a drunkard. The great service he had rendered to me kept prominent in my mind the nobler attributes of his nature; but I could not conceal from myself the simple truth that he was a worthless fellow. I had talked to him very faithfully, but with no result whatever, for he only laughed at me. I do not mean to say that I "preached" to him, or anything of that sort; but as the events of our intimacy brought the topics to our attention, I expressed my convictions without reserve.

I could not believe that he was a bad young man at heart, and I was satisfied that much of his eccentricity was mere affectation, as it generally is with everybody. I honestly and sincerely desired to do him good, and the best thing I could do would be to give him higher views of life than he entertained, to help him to anchor his hopes upon the solid foundation of moral and religious principle. But I had only a day to remain in New York, for the steamer sailed on Wednesday, and we arrived on Monday night. I was not afraid to associate with him, and while I tried to do my duty by him, I also carefully avoided the errors of the Pharisee and the hypocrite.

We had taken a room together in the hotel, and neither of us waked till ten o'clock in the forenoon, for it was four when we retired in the morning. Larry worked half an hour on his pants, which had been somewhat damaged in the water the day before. He had a small valise, from which he took a shirt with extravagant frills on the bosom, and completed his elaborate toilet with the nicest care. I was tired of waiting for him, long before he had finished his labors, and went down into the dining-room to order our breakfast. I seated myself at the table opposite a gentleman of fifty, at whose side sat a beautiful and very interesting young lady of eighteen, doubtless his daughter.

The gentleman seemed to be very sad and nervous, and to some extent the lady had the same appearance, though I saw that she was striving to be cheerful and happy. I looked at her as much as I dared, for there was something very pleasing about her. While I was casting occasional glances at her, she told the gentleman she would go to her room, and get ready to go out. She left the hall just as Larry entered with a copy of the Herald in his hand. He looked at her earnestly, and turned to gaze at her as she passed out of the room.

"That's a stunning pretty girl," said he, in a low tone, as he seated himself at my side.

"Hush! That's her father," I whispered, nodding towards the gentleman on the other side of the table, who seemed to be absorbed in his own gloomy thoughts, and paid no attention to us.

"She is the prettiest girl I ever laid eyes on," added Larry, with enthusiasm, but in a low whisper.

"What's the news?" I asked, in order to change the subject. "I see you have the paper."

"Yes, I always read the Herald at breakfast. I used to stick type on it," he replied, unfolding the sheet. "War in Europe," he continued, reading the head lines under the latest news. "Eighty thousand troops sent into Italy. I should like to be there, and take a hand in that row."

"You don't want to fight — do you?"

"I do; I have a decided taste for it. I fancy there is something in me, and that it will come out in time. I wasn't born to be a jour printer, and when my time comes, I shall be a big man."

"That's all folly, Larry. The only way for a fellow to make anything of himself is to go to work like a man in whatever sphere he may find himself. A jour printer may make a great man of himself as well as any other man; but this soaring after the infinite, and diving into the depths of the unfathomable, are all moonshine."

"You are a philosopher, Phil, of which I am not whom," laughed Larry.

He read the European news while we waited for our breakfast, and as my mother was still at Nice, I was deeply interested in it.

"'Heavy defalcation,'" continued Larry, reading from another column of the paper. "'Our city was thrown into unwonted commotion this morning by the discovery of a heavy defalcation in the Spring Hill Bank. The sudden disappearance of the cashier, Mr. Luther Fennimore, who has hitherto borne an irreproachable character in the city, suggested an examination of the affairs of the bank, which unfortunately resulted in furnishing the most conclusive evidence that a systematic course of fraud had been practised upon the directors for several years. The amount of the defalcation cannot be less than one hundred thousand dollars, and it is believed that the bank will be obliged to go into liquidation.

"'Mr. Fennimore has heretofore enjoyed the entire confidence of the directors, and of the community, and it is painful to know that one who has been so highly respected could descend to the abyss of crime. Mr. Fennimore is a widower, with an only daughter, a beautiful young lady, highly educated and accomplished, and her father's error will be a crushing blow to her. She has been on a visit to a friend in New York city for several weeks, and it is believed that her unfortunate but guilty father will endeavor to see her. Officers have been sent to New York to intercept him if he attempts to leave the country in the Cunard steamer of Wednesday. The sympathies of the public —' Confound the sympathies of the public!" exclaimed Larry, as the waiter brought in our breakfast; and he threw down the paper.

"Why don't you finish the article? I am anxious to hear the rest of it," I interposed.

"Read for yourself, Phil. I never wait my breakfast for the sympathies of the public," answered Larry, taking a large piece of steak from the dish.

When my friend began to read this article, I noticed that the elderly gentleman opposite me suddenly turned very pale. I saw that his lips quivered, and his whole frame was convulsed. He struggled to appear indifferent, but his efforts were only partially successful. I observed him with no little interest, and without seeming to watch him, I scrutinized his looks and actions very closely. I was afraid he was the Mr. Luther Fennimore alluded to in the paragraph. If so, he had abundant reason to be gloomy and nervous. I finished the reading of the article; but the rest of it was only to the effect that the sympathies of the public would be entirely with the beautiful and accomplished daughter of the defaulter. For my own part, I pitied him more than her, though he deserved it less, for he had the burden of crime on his soul, which is the heaviest load that a mortal can carry.

While we were at the table the young lady appeared at the door, and the nervous gentleman hastened to join her. He was so agitated that he could hardly walk. When they had gone, Larry indulged in some enthusiastic remarks about the lady, and declared that he should be sure and be at dinner in order to see her again. I asked the waiter who the gentleman was, but he was unable to give his name. At the office I made the same inquiry, and the clerk pointed to " Park Barnard " on the register, and " Miss Goodspeed " under it. Park Barnard was certainly not the name of the defaulter, and the supposition that the lady and gentleman had entered assumed names on the book implied that she was a party to her father's crime, which I was not willing to believe.

I hastened to the steamer office to engage my passage, and took a berth in an unoccupied stateroom well forward, which I promised to pay for in an hour or two. I hoped to have the room to myself, though it was the last one in which at least one berth had not been taken. I then went to the bankers, and received the money on my draft.

Perhaps it would not have been paid if I had not produced a letter from the banker in St. Louis, who gave a full description of me, in order to avoid this difficulty. With the money I bought a letter of credit, for general use in Europe, for four hundred pounds, and had enough left to pay my passage, and purchase twenty sovereigns in gold, for use before I reached London.

Larry Grimsby went with me to all the places my business required me to visit, and was interested in all that was said and done. He inquired particularly in regard to the method of obtaining funds in Europe, which I explained as well as I was able in so short a time. When I inquired in regard to the terms for the letter of credit, the clerk handed me two or three blank forms. They were signed by the banking firm, but contained no other writing. I concluded that the members of the firm were absent from the city, and had signed these blanks to enable the clerks to do business in this line during their absence. Larry picked up one of them, and read it with interest, while I examined another. The terms were satisfactory to me, and the letter of credit was filled out; I signed it in the margin, and placed it in my pocket-book with other valuable papers. I saw the clerk pick up one or more of the blanks as we left the office. After paying for my passage, and purchasing my sovereigns, we made a visit to the steamer in which I was to cross the Atlantic. I saw my room, and was satisfied with it.

"I wish I was going with you, Phil," said Larry, as we left the ship.

"I wish you were," I replied.

"See here; it is dinner time, Phil," added he, as the clock on Trinity struck the hour.

We hastened to the hotel, and arrived only a little late; but my friend was sorely disappointed when he found that the pretty young lady was not at the table. Neither she nor her father appeared, and we did not see them again at the hotel. After dinner Larry left me to call upon some of his friends. Suspecting that his New York associates were like himself, I declined to go with him. He told me that one of them owed him thirty and another ten dollars, borrowed money, which he hoped to collect; and I was still less inclined to go with him, if it was to be a dunning expedition. I begged him not to drink anything, for he might meet the young lady at the hotel in the evening. He only laughed, and made no promises.

I spent the afternoon in completing the preparations for my voyage. Long before dark Larry returned to the hotel. To my surprise he was not tipsy, and I could not detect even the smell of liquor about him.

"Have you seen the young lady?" he asked.

"No; we will ask about her at the office."

We did so, and learned that the gentleman was quite sick, and that she was attending to his wants. Larry went out again in the evening, but returned before ten o'clock.

"Not a drop, Phil," said he. "I haven't drank anything to-day."

"I suppose you don't feel any the worse for it."

"No; I can't say that I do; but it is hard work to meet your friends and not drink with them."

"Don't do it, Larry, however hard it may be. The idea of a young fellow like you, only nineteen years old, drinking liquor, is absurd. You are almost sure to die a drunkard, if you keep on."

"O, I can take care of myself; but just for a

joke, I thought I would knock off for a while; I always took something before when I had any money; but as I didn't have any, more than half the time, I couldn't always drink, unless some good fellow treated me. But I don't often let a fellow treat me, unless I have the money to retaliate with."

"I hope you will keep up the joke for a year, at least."

"Perhaps I shall; I don't know."

"To-morrow morning I must leave you, as you are aware; but I hope I shall see you again. Will you write to me, Larry, in care of the bankers?" I asked, giving him the address.

"With all my heart, if the circumstances permit," laughed he.

"Tell me where you are; I will answer your letter."

My friend treated the matter very lightly, and with much indifference. We slept as well as usual that night, and I was up early in the morning. I routed out my companion, and we took an early breakfast.

"I think I will pay my bill, for I shall not stay here after you are gone," said Larry, when I called for my account.

"I should think you would get into some good boarding-house, and go to work at once, so that you may always find a dollar in your pocket when you fish for one," I added.

"Your advice shall be considered."

I engaged a car-man to take my trunk over to the city, and Larry, with his little valise in his hand, walked down to the ferry with me. I wondered that he should be so absurd as to carry it over and back, when he could just as well leave it at the hotel; but he insisted upon having his own way. Already there was a crowd on the wharf when we went on board of the ship. Carriages were arriving and departing, and great piles of baggage were conveyed on board. I had my trunk carried to my room, and went down myself, to ascertain whether I was to be alone or not. Larry went with me, and placed his valise in the upper berth. No other passenger appeared, and I proposed to go on deck to see the exciting scenes attending the departure of an ocean steamer.

"Better not leave your valise there, Larry," I suggested. "You may not have time to come down after it, when the order to leave the ship is given."

"My valise has taken passage for Liverpool," laughed he.

"Your valise?"

"Yes; but I have concluded to go with it, in order to take care of it."

"You don't mean to say that you are going to Liverpool — do you?"

"I do," he replied, producing his ticket.

I was confounded by this evidence of his intention, and for certain reasons I was not altogether pleased.

CHAPTER IV.

IN WHICH PHIL WALKS ABOUT THE DECK, AND FINDS ANOTHER GRIMSBY.

I WAS startled by the announcement of Larry Grimsby, that he intended to go to Liverpool in the steamer. As he had his ticket, he had evidently paid his fare, and I had no right to interfere, even if I had been disposed to do so. Certainly I had some selfish fears, which annoyed me not a little. I could not exactly understand where he had obtained money enough to pay for his passage; but I concluded that he had collected the whole or a portion of the forty dollars due him from his former associates in the city. But even if he had added forty dollars to the hundred I had given him, he had plainly expended nearly every dollar in his possession for the purchase of his ticket.

When he landed in Europe he would not have

anything to pay his expenses, and I feared that my exchequer would be required to foot his bills as well as my own. Grateful as I was to him for the valuable service he had rendered me, I could hardly afford to pay his expenses; and when we were together in a foreign land, I did not see how I could refuse to do so, as long as my money lasted. After all, had he not saved my life beyond the possibility of a doubt? With this view, I thought I could not do too much for him, even if I gave him all the money I had in the world. I was determined, therefore, not to worry about him; at least not till I understood his plans better.

We went on deck after securing our seats at the table in the saloon. We walked about, and looked at everybody and everything. I was interested in the busy scene around me, and excited by the prospect before me. Larry took everything as coolly as though he had crossed the ocean a dozen times.

"Hallo, Chaplin!" exclaimed he, as he encountered a rather disagreeable-looking man near the smoke-stack.

"Hist, Larry! Don't mention my name here," replied the person addressed.

"Why not? Do you want to cut an old friend?"

"By no means; but don't mention my name, if you please," added Chaplin, with an expressive wink.

"Certainly not, if you say so; but I am sorry you are ashamed of your name."

"It isn't that, Larry. The fact of it is, I'm in the shadow business just now," replied Chaplin, in a low tone.

"Is that so? This is my particular friend, Phil Farringford."

I shook hands with him, but I did not repeat his name, after the expressive warning not to do so.

"He's in the shadow business," laughed Larry.

"Pray, what's the shadow business?" I asked, having never heard the expression before.

"Don't you know, Phil? He is a detective. He is on the lookout for some rogue who will try to leave in this steamer. Isn't that so, my chap?"

"Just so; big game, too."

"I suppose you won't mind telling me what it is."

"No; it's a bank cashier; but don't mention it."

"Not a word."

"Very likely you read about it in the papers," added Chaplin.

"The one with the highly educated and accomplished daughter — is that the one?"

"The same; he's booked for this steamer; but he won't come on board till the last minute. I'm stationed here, where I can see every one that comes down the wharf. Keep your eyes open, and you may see some fun."

I did not think there could be any fun in seeing a poor wretch arrested for his crime, especially if the anguish of his innocent daughter was to be a part of the spectacle. But I was interested in the case, and when the defaulter appeared, I half expected to see the tremulous gentleman whom I had met at the breakfast table the day before. After talking with the detective a few moments, we continued our walk.

"You know that man, Larry?" I said, wishing to learn more about him.

"Yes; he used to be a printer, and I worked with him," replied my friend. "He's in mean business now; but I think he's up to it."

"Why mean business?"

"Well, it is mean to dog people's steps, and set

traps to catch them. I wouldn't do it to save my body from starvation," continued Larry, explaining the business more in detail.

"I suppose he is sure to catch this man, if he attempts to leave in this ship."

"No doubt of it. There are three or four of them on the wharf and in the vessel."

"By the way, Larry, I fancy we have seen this defaulter," I added.

"No!"

"In my opinion it is the gentleman who was with the young lady at the Western Hotel."

"You don't mean it!"

"Of course I may be mistaken, but I certainly think so;" and I explained the grounds of my belief.

"If I thought he was the father of that stunning pretty girl, I'd help him off, if I could."

"That would not be right," I replied, shaking my head.

"Why not? These banks are sponging shops; they rob the people of their money, and this cashier only paid them off in their own coin."

"Wrong, all wrong. The banks are perfectly proper institutions, and the cashier had no right to take what did not belong to him. Your argument is utterly ridiculous."

"Perhaps it is; I'm no philosopher," laughed he. "I'm going below to get a handkerchief. I'll be with you again in a moment."

I saw him descend the steps, and I walked forward, deeply interested in the exciting scene around me. I passed the "shadow," who still had his eyes fixed on the wharf, where carriages were bringing passengers for the steamer. I continued my walk to the bow, where, as I was turning to retrace my steps, I encountered Larry, as I supposed.

"I thought you went below," I remarked, halting in front of the person addressed. "Did you see Mr. Fennimore and his daughter?"

"I beg your pardon," replied he.

A second glance at him assured me I had made a blunder; but certainly the person bore a marvellous resemblance to my friend. If I had observed his dress before I spoke to him, I might have avoided the blunder.

"Excuse me; I thought it was Mr. Grimsby," I apologized.

"Indeed, sir, that is my name," added the

young man, evidently much perplexed at my conduct.

"But not the Mr. Grimsby with whom I am acquainted, though you look very much like him."

The voice and manner of the speaker were quite different from Larry's, though, looking at his face only, I was not surprised at my mistake. A close scrutiny of his features and expression, however, revealed some points of difference. His dress and manner were decidedly English.

"I beg your pardon," added the stranger; "but you mentioned a gentleman with whom I am connected; my uncle, indeed — Mr. Fennimore."

"I do not even know the person of whom I spoke; but as you seem to be an Englishman, probably he is not the Mr. Fennimore who is your uncle. I allude to the bank defaulter, for whom the officers are just now in search."

"A bank defaulter!" exclaimed he; and I was afraid, after all, that I had "put my foot into it."

"I merely read about the matter in the newspaper," I replied.

"Of course it cannot be my uncle, then, who is coming on board by the post steamer; but it's a bit strange that we have so many people with the same names."

I conversed a few moments with him on indifferent topics, and then resumed my walk. The bells began to ring violently, and an officer ordered all but the passengers to go ashore. The great hawsers were cast off, and the wheels began to turn. I passed the "shadow," and saw he had no intention of leaving the steamer.

"Do you go to Liverpool with us?" I asked.

"No; a small steamer brings off the mails, and very likely my man will come off in her."

This was doubtless the boat which the English Grimsby called the "post steamer." Of course, as he was from England, the defaulter could not be his uncle. I paced the deck again, bestowing my last look upon the city of New York. Hundreds of people, on the wharf and on the steamer, were waving their adieus with hats and handkerchiefs, and I tried to be a little sentimental. I wondered why Larry did not come up to witness this interesting scene; but I saw nothing of him.

"We are off," said some one near me.

I turned, and found that the remark was addressed to me. As I did so, I recognized the

English Grimsby with a young lady on his arm. I was not a little startled when I discovered that she was the same one I had seen at the Western Hotel.

"I beg your pardon," said Mr. Grimsby; "but I desire very much to see the person for whom you mistook me."

"He is not on deck just at this moment," I replied; "but I will bring him to you as soon as he comes up."

"Thank you. I'm curious about the matter, especially as you mentioned my uncle's name. I beg your pardon, but I haven't the pleasure of your name."

"Mr. Farringford. Philip Farringford."

"Thank you, Mr. Farringford. You have mine, and now we are even. This is Miss Fennimore, my cousin."

The young lady bowed rather coldly, as though she did not quite approve the conduct of her cousin in introducing her to a mere chance acquaintance.

"This is a beautiful day we have to commence our voyage," I added.

"Very fine," she answered, somewhat haughtily.

Finding that my company was not particularly agreeable to her, I touched my hat, bowed, and retired. I wanted to see Larry then, for the request of Grimsby would afford me an opportunity of introducing him to both. He was not on deck yet, and I was going below to seek him, when the steamer's wheels stopped, and the mail-boat came alongside. I was curious to see what was done, and I anticipated an exciting scene when the defaulter came on board. Though I could not explain it, I was satisfied that the uncle of Grimsby was the person for whom the officers were seeking. The haughty young lady must suffer a degree of anguish she had never known before. I pitied her, but I could not leave the deck while this terrible scene was impending. The mails were brought on board, and then the baggage. I looked eagerly for the gentleman who had been so nervous at the hotel when Larry read the news. He did not appear, and the small steamer was ready to cast off. Chaplin was disconcerted. I saw him in consultation with several others, who, I concluded, were "shadows," like himself. The bells rang, and the officers shouted; but the detectives were not ready to leave the ship.

They spoke to the impatient captain, and then went into the saloon. I followed them, curious to know what was to be done. They scrutinized all the passengers in the cabin, and then went below. I saw them looking into all the state-rooms.

"This is his room," said Chaplin, at the one next to mine, "or at least the one engaged for Mr. Park Barnard."

There were some trunks in it, but no passengers. I found that my room was locked, and the shadow knocked at the door.

"Who's there?" demanded Larry.

"Open the door, Larry," I replied, taking the matter out of the hands of the officers.

"Hold on a minute, Phil. I'm mending my trousers."

Chaplin laughed, and said he knew that voice.

"Is this your room?" he asked, turning to me.

"Yes; Larry and I have it together," I answered.

"Is there any other person in there?"

"There are only two berths; Larry has one, and I have the other."

"That's all right," added Chaplin, as he and his companions passed on to the next room.

I followed them, as did half a dozen others, including the chief steward. The search was a fruitless one. Mr. Fennimore could not be found, and the " shadows " were satisfied that he was not on board.

"He was afraid to show himself after that article in the newspapers," said Chaplin to one of his fellows. "That newspaper correspondent ought to be hung."

They went on board of the mail-boat, and when it had cast off, the great wheels of the steamer began to turn again, and we were actually commencing the voyage. Miss Fennimore and Grimsby were on the quarter-deck, and I went below again to see Larry, after we had passed the Narrows. The door of our room was still fastened, and I knocked.

"Who is it?" called Larry.

"Open the door," I replied.

"Hold on a little while — will you, Phil?"

"Can't you let me in now?"

"Are you alone?"

"Yes."

I thought the last was rather an odd question, and I did not see the point of it; but he opened the door, and I stepped in.

"What in the world are you about, Larry?" I asked.

"I have to do my own mending," laughed he; "and I was busy at a job that comes under that head."

"But why didn't you go on deck, and see the fun? We have passed through the Narrows, and the view was worth seeing."

"Confound the view! I have seen it a hundred times before now."

"There is a young fellow on board — an Englishman — that looks like you, Larry; so much so that I spoke to him, thinking it was you. He wants to see you; and there is a certain young lady with him."

"Precisely so," he replied, exhibiting no surprise. "And I was spoken to by a gentleman who thought I was somebody else. He called me Miles. By the way, Phil, have the cops all gone?"

"The what?"

"The shadows — you know."

"Every one of them. They were disappointed, and declared that the newspaper article you read had defeated their plans."

"Perhaps it did."

"The officers searched the steamer before they left."

"I know they did," chuckled Larry.

"How did you know, when you were mending your trousers, locked up in your room?"

"I didn't mend them much," he replied, glancing at his berth with an expression so significant that I could not help doing the same.

In the berth, with his head resting upon his hand, was Mr. Luther Fennimore, the bank defaulter; and I realized what my unprincipled companion had been doing. I was startled, as though an apparition had suddenly burst upon my view.

CHAPTER V.

IN WHICH PHIL LISTENS TO THE DEFAULTER'S STORY, AND BECOMES BETTER ACQUAINTED WITH BLANCHE FENNIMORE.

THE steamer had discharged her pilot, and was well away from the land, when I discovered Mr. Fennimore in my state-room. Though I believe, most earnestly, that every man should mind his own business, I am satisfied that under the specious pretence of doing so, many people connive at knavery. I could not help asking myself whether any responsibility rested upon me for the escape of the defaulter. As I had made the discovery of his presence in my room only after the ship was clear of the land, I could not believe that any guilt attached to me. I do not think that bank defaulters are any the less guilty because they have moved in good society; and certainly, if I had known that Mr. Fennimore was on board, I would have done what I could to bring him to justice for his crime.

Miles Grimsby had told me that his uncle would come off to the steamer in the boat with the mails, and I was very much surprised to find that he was on board. Just before I went below, I had seen Miles and Miss Fennimore walking on the hurricane deck. I wondered now whether she knew all the time that her father was on board. If she expected him to come off in the mail-boat, she would naturally have been very much alarmed at his non-appearance. I had not noticed any demonstration on her part, and I was driven to the conclusion that she knew he was in the ship. I did not see how the defaulter could have eluded the officers without the assistance of Larry. The daughter did not seem to trouble herself about the safety of her father, and I still regarded her as innocent of all knowledge of his crime.

Mr. Fennimore lay in the upper berth, which had been appropriated to Larry's use. His head rested upon his hand, and he had evidently been engaged in conversation with my room-mate. His hair was disarranged, and his toilet much disturbed, and I concluded, from the appearance of the bed-clothing, that he had been concealed beneath it. He was still very nervous, and wore the same anxious expression as when I had first seen him at the table of the hotel. I glanced at him, and then at Larry. My friend chuckled, and evidently thought he had done a clever thing in outwitting the officers, and in throwing dust into my eyes.

"Come in, Phil," said Larry, after I had regarded the situation in silence for a moment.

"This room seems to be pretty well occupied already," I replied.

"Room enough for one more, my dear fellow. Come in, and make yourself at home — as though you belonged here."

"I had an idea that I did belong here; but I begin to think I do not," I added.

"Come in, young man, if you please," said Mr. Fennimore. "I am ready to leave your room now; but I should like to speak with you a few moments before I go."

I entered the room, and seated myself on the narrow sofa under the port. Larry shut the door, and bolted it.

"It seems, young man, that you know my secret," continued the defaulter.

"I know it now; I only suspected it before," I answered.

"We met at the hotel, I think."

"I saw you and your daughter there. When my friend here read the article in the Herald about the bank defaulter, I saw that you were very nervous, and trembled violently. I concluded from this circumstance, and the description of your daughter, that you were the person."

"It would be useless, even if it were necessary, for me to attempt to conceal the fact that I am the person — Mr. Fennimore, the bank defaulter," he replied, with a shudder, as if the acknowledgment of his crime wrung his very soul.

"You entered your name at the hotel as Park Barnard," I added.

"I did."

"Does your daughter know that you are on board?" I inquired.

"She does; she came with me. I knew from the article which was in the paper that I should be closely watched, and we came on board before six o'clock this morning. I bribed porters and servants; I told them I was sick,— as, indeed, I am,— and had just reached the city. A steward showed me my room, which is the next to this. I explained that I did not wish to be disturbed, and asked him not to tell any one that I was on board. No one came near me, and I believed that I was safe till this young man, whom I took to be my nephew when I spoke to him, assured me of my mistake, and kindly aided me. He concealed me in his bed, and covered me with bags and valises, in such a way that he declared I was entirely safe."

"But the officers didn't even look in, Phil, thanks to your assistance," chuckled Larry.

"They would have come in, if I had suspected that anything was wrong," I replied.

"Come, come! Don't be ugly, after you have done a good thing for a fellow."

"I see that I have not your sympathies," added the anxious occupant of the upper berth.

"Personally I have no ill will against you; but I would not willingly aid any man in concealing a crime, like robbing a bank. Does your nephew know that you are here?"

"Probably Blanche has told him by this time."

" Blanche ? "

" My daughter. I told Miles yesterday that Blanche would come on board with a friend, and I should join her by the mail-boat."

" Does Miles or your daughter know that you are a defaulter?" I asked.

" Certainly not; whatever becomes of me, I hope they will never know it," added Mr. Fennimore, with a convulsive start.

" Was the statement in the paper true, that you had taken a hundred thousand dollars from the bank?" I asked.

" It was. Twenty-five years ago I was a merchant, and a successful one. At the age of twenty-three I was admitted as the junior partner of a large house in New York. I went to Europe frequently, and in England married Sara Groveland, the daughter of Sir Hale Groveland, Knight. Miles Grimsby, the father of the young man on board, who resembles our friend here so strongly, and the son of Sir Philip Grimsby, Baronet, married another daughter of Sir Hale. I was fortunate, but I was extravagant. I intended that my wife should live in a style equal to that of her titled relatives in England; and she did. One of the senior partners of our firm died, the other retired, and the business came into my hands. But it had lost its controlling minds, though I believed myself fully competent to manage it, even better than my late seniors. I was mistaken, and in a couple of years I made a disastrous failure. I tried again, with no better success. I was poor — very poor. I had nothing, and no one would give me credit. My wife never reproached me, but my reverses preyed upon her spirits, and she died, leaving me an only daughter. Perhaps affliction chastened me for a time. With the aid of powerful friends, I obtained the situation of cashier of the Lowerville Bank.

"I had no vices, and I was respected in the community. I kept house for my daughter's sake, and gave her a very expensive education. As she grew older, I had parties for her benefit; and spoiled by the luxury and extravagance of my earlier years, I exceeded my income, and ran in debt. To avoid trouble outside, I used the funds of the bank, intending to reduce my expenses, and return the sums I had appropriated. Instead of being able to diminish my expenditures, they continued to increase, until I found that I owed the bank nearly fifty thousand dollars. I was appalled and terrified by the extent of my defalcation. I could not hope to make it good. The officers of the bank had unlimited confidence in me, and I had the villain's art to conceal the frauds. But I worried day and night about my situation. Sleep was almost a stranger to my eyelids, and my health failed. I felt that I must soon die, and I trembled when I thought that a week's illness and absence from the bank might expose its affairs and my crime to the world. I could not endure the idea of leaving my daughter only a legacy of poverty and crime, and I determined, before it was too late, to flee to another country.

"Blanche, like a true and loving daughter, was sadly troubled about my failing health, and I spoke to her of going to Europe for its restoration. My sister and her son Miles had spent the winter in Virginia, for her health, and a month ago came New York, to visit friends there. Blanche was also invited, and deeming this a good opportunity to carry out my plan, I told her to accept the invitation, and that we would go to England with the Grimsbys in May. She went to the city, and did not again return to Lowerville. I took fifty thousand dollars of the funds of the bank, and then closed its doors for the last time, on the day before I saw you at the hotel. Before dark I was in New York, and took Blanche from the house of her friends, on the plea that the hotel was nearer the steamer. Before it was known to the public at large, I had changed my funds into gold and Bank of England notes, for I dared not trust them in a bill of exchange. The money is in this small valise," said he, raising the portmanteau in the berth. "The article you read frightened me terribly; and I am so ill now that I can hardly stand up."

"Then none of your friends with you know what you have done?" I asked.

"No; nor suspect it. I hope to reach some retired place in Italy or Germany, where I may live in peace and penitence," said he, gloomily.

"Penitence!" I exclaimed. "I should say there could be no such thing till you had restored your ill-gotten wealth."

"I cannot starve."

"Better starve than be dishonest."

"But my daughter?"

"I am sure, if she knew the whole truth, she would not permit you to retain a penny of the stolen money."

"You are right, Mr. Farringford," replied the defaulter, with a groan of real anguish.

"Don't be too stiff, Phil," interposed Larry. "Blanche shall never know anything about this matter."

"Mr. Farringford is right; he is an honest young man; and if he knew how much I have suffered, he would pity me."

"I do pity you now; but I should respect you more, if you gave up the stolen money."

"I have not the courage to do that; but I feel quite ill, and I wish to go to my own room now."

Larry and I assisted him to his state-room, and saw him made as comfortable as possible.

"You will not betray me to my daughter, Mr. Farringford — will you?" pleaded he.

"I don't know what to do. I should feel as though I had a guilty knowledge of your crime, if I assisted in concealing it. But I shall not make your daughter unhappy, if I can avoid it. We will drop the matter now, if you please."

"Will one of you ask Blanche to come to me? I feel very ill indeed, and I wonder she does not come down."

"I will go, and Larry may stay with you till she comes," I replied, leaving the room.

I went to the hurricane deck. The steamer had some time before begun to roll in the long swells of the ocean, though the weather was mild and pleasant. I found Blanche Fennimore extended upon a seat, looking very pale. She was seasick, and this fully explained her continued absence from her father. Mrs. Grimsby, her aunt, lay near her in the same situation, and Miles was taking care of both of them.

"Both ill," said Miles, as I paused near the sufferers.

"So I perceive."

"Have you seen my uncle, or don't you know him?"

"He is in his room, quite ill."

"He is very feeble; he told me he should come off in the post steamer; but my cousin says they came on board early in the morning, because he was so ill."

"He wished me to find his daughter."

"Do you speak of my father?" said Miss Fennimore, raising her head a little.

"Yes; he is quite sick, and desires to see you. I have just assisted him to his berth. I will tell him you are sick," I replied.

"No; I will go to him. Poor father! he is very feeble, and his is not seasickness."

She rose from her reclining posture on the seat, and a roll of the ship would have thrown her down, if Miles had not caught her arm.

"I will take you down," said he.

"Don't leave me, Miles," groaned Mrs. Grimsby.

"My mother is very bad; perhaps Mr. Farringford will assist you, Blanche."

"Certainly," I replied, promptly offering my arm, which she took.

Being an old sailor, I was entirely at home on the uneasy deck, and safely conducted my fair charge down to the main deck.

"Do you feel any worse for moving?" I asked.

"Yes; I can hardly stand; let me sit down for a moment."

I conducted her to a sofa, and then went to the cabin for a lemon, which I offered to her. She gasped her thanks, and following my direction, swallowed a considerable portion of the lemon juice. In a few moments she declared that she felt a little better, and was ready to go below.

"Is my father worse?" she asked.

"I fear he is; and I am afraid it is not sea-sickness," I replied.

"No; he has been in failing health for a long time. I hope this journey will help him."

"We have done what we could for him, and my friend is taking care of him now."

"You are very kind, and I thank you greatly. Your friend is very good."

"He is a noble fellow. Only three days ago he saved my life at the peril of his own, though I had never seen him before. He is always trying to help some one."

We reached the state-room of Mr. Fennimore, where Larry was still at work over his patient. He had placed the trunks under the lower berth, and put everything in order in the little apartment. I introduced him to Miss Fennimore, as we entered. He received her with extravagant deference, and placed a stool for her use at the side of her father's berth.

"I am glad you have come, Blanche," moaned her father.

"You are very sick, father!" exclaimed she, anxiously.

"I shall soon be better. I missed you very much," he added.

"I found her quite ill with seasickness," I interposed.

"Poor child!" said he. "I hoped she would not be sick; but she was never at sea before."

"I am better now, father," replied she, trying to be cheerful; but I saw that it was very up-hill work.

"I have had a kind friend and nurse in Mr. Grimsby," added the sick man.

"I am very grateful to him. How much he looks like Miles! I am not surprised at the mistake you made, Mr. Farringford."

"I made the same mistake," continued Mr. Fennimore, very feebly.

He seemed to me to be in a dangerous condition, and I advised the calling of the doctor; but the invalid would not consent to it, and Larry and I left him to the tender ministrations of his daughter, asking her to knock on the partition which separated our room from Mr. Fennimore's, if she needed any assistance. We did not dare to say anything about the remarkable events of the day, lest the innocent daughter should overhear it. We busied ourselves for a time in putting the room in order; but in less than half an hour, we heard the knock on the partition.

CHAPTER VI.

IN WHICH PHIL HAS A MELANCHOLY PASSAGE ACROSS THE ATLANTIC.

LARRY and I returned to the state-room of Mr. Fennimore. Blanche was still very pale, but her anxiety about her father seemed to have overcome her own tendency to seasickness. Possibly the lemon which she still used had some effect. She said nothing about herself; all her thought was for her father, who was suffering severe pain, probably increased by the uneasy motion of the ship. Mr. Fennimore had consented that the surgeon should be called, and I went for him. He made a careful examination of the patient, and prescribed medicines for him. He looked very serious, but he expressed no decided opinion in regard to the result.

Though I had had very little experience in sickness, I believed that the defaulter had worn

himself out with the anxiety which his crime produced. He was very feeble when I first saw him, and in a state of tremulous anxiety. I had no doubt that often, when he should have been in his bed at home, he had gone to the bank, goaded thither by a fear of discovery. He had evidently sapped out the fountains of vitality in his system, and I felt that crime was the cruelest taskmaster in the world. His safety for a time seemed to be assured as soon as the steamer was in blue water. The excitement which had strained his nerves to their utmost tension was partially removed, and there seemed to be nothing now to sustain him. As soon as the pressure was abated he sank under the change.

I went out when the doctor did, and asked him a question in regard to the patient. After I had told him that the sick man was not my relative, he spoke with more freedom. He declared that Mr. Fennimore was a very sick man; one who had probably exhausted all his vitality in attending too closely to his business; there was nothing left of him. He declined to express an opinion in regard to the result of the sickness, but said he considered the invalid in a very dangerous condition, and that the ship was the worst place in the world for him.

I cannot follow the case into its details. Mr. Fennimore grew worse every day, and even every hour. Poor Blanche was almost helpless, for the sea was rough, and she was able to do very little. Larry was with the sick man day and night, nursing him as tenderly and carefully as though the sufferer had been his own father. Mrs. Grimsby was still down with seasickness, and unable to leave her berth. I did all that Larry would permit me to do, which was hardly three or four hours' service at night while he slept. I regarded him as a wonderful fellow, for while he appeared to have no high moral or religious principle, he was willing to wear himself out in the service of others. He kept Blanche from her father's room as much as possible, and two or three times every day I walked with her on deck. She talked of nothing but her father, and I could say very little to comfort her, for I knew that the doctor now regarded the case as almost hopeless. I told Larry to walk with Miss Fennimore; but, singular being that he was, he would never do it, though he made no secret to me of his admiration, and even his love, for the young lady. He kept his post at the sick bed of her father.

After one of these walks with Blanche, on the sixth day from New York, I returned with her to Mr. Fennimore's room. Larry followed me into our own apartment, leaving the daughter to take care of the sufferer. He looked very serious and strange to me, and I was sure that he had something to say, before he opened his mouth.

"Phil," said he, looking into my face, but quickly lowering his gaze to the floor.

"Well, Larry?"

He looked at me, then through the port, and on the floor.

"What were you going to say?" I asked.

"Did you ever pray, Phil?" he added, as if speaking with a desperate effort.

"Certainly. I do so every day; and I hope you do."

"I never did such a thing in all my life. I always looked upon it as buncombe and humbug; but I am beginning to change my mind. I never saw a man suffer so much in his mind as Mr. Fennimore does. It is really horrible. You were right about robbing banks, and such things. It don't pay. I would rather live on half rations for forty years, than endure what Fennimore suffers in ten minutes. He asked me to pray with him, while you were walking with Blanche. He could hardly speak, but he was in earnest. I told him I couldn't do it; had never done such a thing in my life; but that I would speak to you about it."

"Isn't there a clergyman on board, among the passengers?"

"That's what I suggested to him; but he does not wish to see any strangers. Can't you pray with him, Phil? It will do him a power of good, I think."

"I will, if he desires it," I answered, taking my Bible from the shelf.

"Between you and me, Phil, you will be too late if you don't do it soon," whispered Larry, very seriously. "I don't believe he will hold out another day."

"I will go to him at once," I replied, and left the room.

I had hardly entered his apartment before Mr. Fennimore, in a scarcely audible voice, introduced the subject upon which Larry had spoken to me.

I saw that he was suffering terribly in view of the near approach of death.

Blanche was weeping, and I was confident that he had told her he had not long to live. I had never before seen greater human agony than was depicted on his wan face, and I have not since; and the mental anguish was vastly greater than the physical. Larry soon followed me, and then, with difficulty, Mr. Fennimore asked his daughter to leave him for a few moments. Under ordinary circumstances, this would have been a strange request; but I understood the sufferer's motives, and I seconded his desire, though I do not believe, if the whole truth in regard to her father's crime had been revealed to her at that moment, it would have checked the current of her filial love. I would not have impaired her confidence in him for all the world. Larry gently led her from the state-room.

"Pray for me, Mr. Farringford," gasped the invalid, with a violent effort.

"Shall I read you a few verses from the New Testament first?" I asked.

"Anything that will tell me whether God can forgive one who has sinned as I have sinned," groaned he.

I was familiar enough with the sacred writings to find the passages most appropriate to his condition. Then I talked to him for a few minutes. I repeated what I had read, that Christ on the cross had assured the repentant malefactor of his pardon. I urged upon him the necessity of making all the restitution in his power for the crime he had committed.

"I will! I will!" exclaimed he, with all the vehemence his feebleness would permit. "Take that valise, Mr. Farringford, and return the money to the bank. I can do no more than this, and my daughter may suffer from want because I do this. O God, forgive me for Christ's sake!" groaned he, as the scene of his guilt weighed down his soul, now ready to wing its flight from the mortal body. Deeply moved by what I saw and heard, I knelt down before his berth, and prayed for him with all the earnestness which my pitying heart demanded of me. Nothing more sincere had ever passed my lips, and as I proceeded, the penitent defaulter uttered the most devout invocations for pardon. I finished, and then repeated to him some of the hymns I had learned, which illustrate the mercy and forgiveness of God to the truly penitent.

They comforted him even more than the prayer. But he was exhausted, and could no longer utter a word; yet his face looked more serene and placid. I asked him if he felt more at peace, and he nodded his head. Blanche and Larry returned, but I continued to repeat the hymns to him. I wished I could sing, but I could not. I had heard a party of ladies and gentlemen sing "Nearer, my God, to thee," on Sunday, and I left the cabin to find them. I asked them to sing this hymn near the bedside of the dying man, and they promptly consented. I placed them in the gangway near the door, and then told Mr. Fennimore what I had done. He smiled then — what I had never seen him do before. The ladies and gentlemen sang the beautiful hymn in tender and subdued tones. The dying man listened as though it were the music of a choir of angels hovering over his couch. Repeatedly he smiled as he pressed the hand of Blanche, and I realized that he was at peace.

The doctor frequently came to the state-room. From the beginning he had done everything it was possible for a good physician to do. Among the passengers was an English medical gentleman of considerable celebrity, who was called in for consultation; so we felt that every possible thing had been done for the patient. Mr. Fennimore was calm and peaceful now, and we left him alone with Blanche for a time. Late in the evening he wished to see me again. More by signs than by words he made me understand that I was to open the valise and take therefrom his ill-gotten wealth. I did so.

"Send the money to the bank," said he, in a hardly audible whisper.

I promised to do what he desired, and I realized that this act was a great comfort and consolation to him.

"Did Blanche know you had this money?" I inquired.

"No; no one knew it. Send it back — I shall die in peace."

With a heavy sense of responsibility resting upon me, I placed the large sum in my trunk. I did not deem it advisable even to mention the matter to Larry. Contrary to all our expectations, Mr. Fennimore lived two days longer; and I think his life was prolonged by the peace he had found in penitence and pardon. Several times a day I read the Scriptures to him, and prayed with him. The singers sang several hymns near his room, to which he listened in enraptured silence. Blanche was more reconciled when her father became so gentle and peaceful. She was tolerably calm in his presence, but she wept incessantly when away from him. The passengers were full of sympathy, and the poor girl had no lack of comforters among those of her own sex who had passed through a similar experience.

On the ninth day from New York, the green shores of Ireland were in sight; but Mr. Fennimore was rapidly sinking. After dinner, the party of singers had just finished the last line of "I would not live alway," when Larry whispered that a sudden change had come over the sufferer. I went to his berth. His face was calm and placid as the sleep of an infant. He had passed away. The last sweet strains of earthly music which soothed his mortal sense had been mingled with those of angelic choirs, as this mortal put on immortality. In spite of his great crime, I could not but believe that all was well with him, for he had thrown himself upon the mercy of God in Christ, and done all he could to atone for his errors. I closed his eyes, and Blanche sank upon the sofa in a paroxysm of grief.

After a time, her aunt led her away, and the chief steward performed the necessary offices upon the remains. It was midnight when we arrived at Queenstown. An order was sent forward, by a passenger, to Liverpool, for an undertaker to make the arrangements for conveying the remains to Bloomridge, in Staffordshire, where the Grimsbys resided.

"Phil, I shall never forget this voyage," said Larry, the next day, as the ship was going up the Channel.

"Neither shall I ever forget it," I replied. "I expected to have a good time on the passage, but it has been one of the saddest seasons of my life."

"That's so; and I have been hard at work most of the time; but I must say I am better satisfied with myself than I ever was before."

"You have behaved nobly, Larry."

"Never mind that. I have seen more of life than I ever dreamed of before. I have been a reckless fellow. I never believed much in religion, goodness, and such kind of things; but after following Mr. Fennimore to the end, I have altered my mind," said he, very seriously. "That man was miserable beyond anything I ever saw or imagined; and I wouldn't rob a bank now, even if I had as good a chance as he had, though I don't know that I have as much conscience as he had."

"I'm glad to see you taking a reasonable view of these things."

"Reasonable! See here, Phil," he added, taking a paper from his pocket and unfolding it.

"What's that?" I asked, curiously.

"Look at it;" and he handed the paper to me.

It was one of the blank forms of a letter of credit, such as I had, with the signature of the banking firm upon it.

"What of it?" I inquired.

"Don't you remember that paper?"

"I don't particularly remember this one."

"When you obtained your letter of credit, you know the clerk handed out two or three of these things."

"O, yes; I remember now; but where did you get this?"

"While the clerk was filling out your letter,

I folded up one of the blanks and put it in my pocket," he replied, looking much ashamed of himself.

"What for? What use can this empty blank be to you?"

"None now," he answered, taking the paper from my hand, tearing it into small pieces with considerable vigor, and then throwing them overboard. "That's all."

"I really don't understand you, Larry," I added, puzzled by his conduct.

"Don't you? Then perhaps you give me credit for being a better fellow than I am. I shall go to work in Liverpool, if I can find a job in a printing office; if not, I shall ship for home as a common sailor."

"I have thought your plans were rather loosely laid, but I don't comprehend you yet."

"You are a little thick, Phil, in some things. You have saved me from — Well, I don't know what you have saved me from."

"I am not aware that I have saved you from anything."

"Yes, you have; you haven't preached much at me; if you had, it would have done me no good. But you have hit me all the harder."

"Tell me what you mean."

"I intended to fill out that blank, draw the money on it, and have a good time in Europe for a year or two," he replied, desperately, as if the confession was too shameful to be made.

I understood him then.

CHAPTER VII.

IN WHICH PHIL AND HIS FRIEND VISIT GRIMSBY HALL, AND ARE PRESENT AT A MELANCHOLY OCCASION.

MY motto from the beginning had been, "Upward and Onward." Perhaps I ought not to say it, but I had distinctly set before myself the purpose of becoming a good and true man, whatever else I was. I made mistakes, many and grievous ones, but I tried to do my duty. I had always been afraid of evil companions, and, as I have before remarked, I did not like the character of Larry Grimsby. He had no high aims, no moral principle, to guide and control his life. But, whatever he had said, I did not believe him capable of the crime he confessed to have meditated.

The blank letter of credit was signed by the banking firm. But filling it out and "uttering" it were no less a crime than if he had added the further act of forging the signature of the bankers. I understood his plan now. He had expended all his money in the purchase of his steamer ticket, and he intended to replenish his exchequer to a liberal extent by drawing on this letter. Probably he considered that being with me, who had a genuine credit, would remove all doubts in regard to his own; indeed, he acknowledged as much to me. But he had destroyed the blank, and announced his intention of going to work, or returning to New York.

"I did not think you would do such a thing," I said, sadly.

"I knew I would, if I got a good chance. But that's all gone by now. After witnessing the sufferings of poor Mr. Fennimore, I would starve rather than do such a thing. I don't like cant, Phil, but my eyes have been opened. I would give all my old boots, if I had any, to be half as good as you are, my boy."

"I hope you will try to be better than I am."

"That's humbug, Phil. You know you are a saint."

"I know that I am a sinner, but I am trying to do right; that is all I can say for myself."

"Never mind, Phil: I don't believe you are a hypocrite. If you had been, you couldn't have done so much for poor Mr. Fennimore. Why, you lifted him right up, and made a new man of him. I believe there is something in religion now. I never thought there was before. I'm going to try to be a better fellow."

"If you try, I know you will succeed. You have a good heart, with noble and generous emotions. You are entirely unselfish, and are willing to wear yourself out in the service of others."

"Thank you, Phil. I always mean to stand by a fellow as long as there is anything left of him."

"All you need is a high moral and religious principle."

"I intend to look into that matter," said he, thoughtfully. "But I suppose we must part as soon as we land."

"I hope not," I replied.

"Of course we must; I haven't ten shillings in the world."

"O, I shall be glad to help you out," I added, warmly.

"No, Phil; you have done enough for me; but

the biggest thing you did was to save me from filling out that blank." .

"But I have not done half so much for you as you have for me."

"There, there; no more of that. I don't want any of your gratitude."

"Yet that was precisely in your own strain. Here are ten sovereigns, Larry; and I won't say another word about what you have done for me, unless you introduce the subject yourself."

"I won't take them," said he, doubtfully, but evidently tempted to do so.

"You must! Would you compel me to leave a good fellow alone in a foreign land without any money in his pocket, when I have plenty?"

"As a loan, Phil, I will take this money, for I feel that I need it; but I solemnly assure you that, if I ever pay any debt before I pay the debt of nature, this shall be the first one," replied Larry, as he slipped the gold into his pocket.

"Don't distress yourself about it, my dear fellow."

Certainly there was enough of good in Larry Grimsby to redeem him from the evil, which he hardly attempted to conceal, but rather made an affectation of displaying.

7

"I don't think I shall distress myself about anything; but I am more likely to obtain a job in London than in Liverpool. I believe your great philosopher, Franklin, was tolerably successful there in my line."

We hardly saw Blanche Fennimore during the day, for she remained with her aunt in the state-room. It was after midnight when the steamer anchored in the Mersey, and few of the passengers went ashore in the boat which came off for the mails and those who desired to land at once. At breakfast Blanche came to the table, the very picture of misery. Larry and I waited in the saloon till she was ready to leave.

"I suppose we must part here, Miss Fennimore," I began, as we met her at the door.

"Part?" she replied.

"We go direct to London."

"You will not leave me now. You must go to Bloomridge with us," she added, in pleading tones. "You were so kind to my poor father and to me, that I cannot endure the thought of parting with you. I hope you will attend my father's funeral. I am sure he would have desired it."

"We did not know what arrangements had

been made, and we have not considered the subject," I answered.

"Let me speak with my aunt about the matter," said she.

She followed her aunt below, and presently Miles Grimsby came to us with an invitation to spend the time till after the funeral at Bloomridge. Though I was in a hurry to reach Italy, I felt obliged to accept the invitation, out of regard to the feelings of poor Blanche.

The undertaker had come on board early in the morning, and the remains of Mr. Fennimore, now placed in a coffin, were conveyed to the tug-steamer. We went on board with Blanche and the Grimsbys, and repaired directly to the Lime Street station; but we were obliged to wait an hour for the train. This afforded me time to attend to the last wishes of the deceased; and I had written a letter on board the steamer to the president of the Lowerville Bank, whose address I had been careful to obtain of Mr. Fennimore, detailing the events which had occurred on the passage. I begged him, for the sake of Blanche, to let the matter rest without further exposure, since the deceased had made all the reparation in his power.

Taking a cab, I drove to the bankers upon whom my letter of credit was issued, and purchased a bill for the full amount intrusted to me by Mr. Fennimore. This I sent in my letter, instructing the bankers to forward the duplicates, which they promised to do. I posted the precious document, and felt that I had discharged a sacred duty.

"Where have you been, Phil?" asked Larry, when I returned to the station.

"To the bankers."

"You robbed yourself when you loaned me the ten pounds."

"Not at all; I did not go to draw money;" and I explained to him what had transpired between Mr. Fennimore and myself in regard to the stolen money.

"Send it all back!" exclaimed he, with no little astonishment.

"Every penny of it — about fifty thousand dollars."

"You didn't say anything to me about this."

"No; it was a matter between Mr. Fennimore and myself; and I thought it had better remain so until the business was finished."

"You were afraid I would steal the money if I knew you had it. I don't blame you; but —"

"I was not afraid you would steal it, and my course saved all argument on the subject. I did not know but you might think it your duty to speak to Blanche or the Grimsbys about the money, and thus complicate the matter."

"Of course I should not have said anything to them."

"You might have spoken of the money without mentioning the crime."

"No, I should not. I might have done it a week ago, but not three days ago. After Mr. Fennimore had ruined himself to obtain this money, his daughter has not a penny to show for it."

"No; but her father died in peace, after he had given me the money, and instructed me to restore it to the rightful owners. That is something to show for giving it up — isn't it?"

"I think it is; and you are right, Phil, as you always are; but I am sorry for poor Blanche, without a red to help herself with."

"Her English friends are wealthy, and she will never want for anything," I replied.

It was late in the day when we arrived at Bloomridge, and took carriages for Grimsby Hall, a mile from the station. Mrs. Grimsby and Miles were warmly welcomed by the family. Blanche was very kindly, and even tenderly, received, for her bereaved condition excited all the sympathies of her friends. After all these welcomes had been given, and condolences extended, Larry and myself were introduced. The family consisted of Sir Philip Grimsby, and his son Miles, who dwelt beneath the paternal roof with his wife, his son Miles, and two daughters.

I had never before seen a live baronet, and I was deeply impressed by his appearance, but more by the fact that he was a baronet. He was rather stiff and haughty in his manners at first, and I regarded him with much deference and humiliation. But Larry did not seem to be awed in the slightest degree, when his turn came to be presented to the old gentleman.

"Eh!" exclaimed the baronet, stepping back, as my friend advanced, in order to survey his features more closely. "What did you say the name was, Miles?" he added, turning to his grandson.

"Mr. Grimsby," replied Miles, apparently amused at the manner of his grandfather.

"Grimsby! Upon my life, he looks like one of us!" added Sir Philip. "I'm glad to see you, Mr. Grimsby."

"Thank you, sir," replied Larry, stepping forward, and extending his hand — a familiarity in which I had not ventured to indulge.

The baronet took the offered hand, but he still continued to regard with the closest scrutiny the face of my friend.

"He looks like you, Miles," added he. "But upon my life, he looks more like your uncle that died. Will you oblige me with your given name, Mr. Grimsby?"

"I'm generally called Larry, sir."

"But that's a nickname."

"It certainly labors under that imputation."

"For what is Larry a nickname, sir?" asked Sir Philip.

"For Lawrence, sir. I was entered on the steamer's passenger list as Lawrence Grimsby," replied Larry, with easy assurance.

"Lawrence Grimsby!" exclaimed the baronet, dropping into a chair, as if overcome by some unexplained emotion.

But he soon appeared to become conscious that

he was acting in an unusual manner, and rose from his chair.

"Gentlemen, you are welcome to Grimsby Hall. We dine at six. Breck, show the gentlemen the rooms prepared for them," he added, turning to a servant.

Each of our apartments, which were connected, was large enough for a ball-room, and furnished in a heavy, substantial, old-fashioned style. Breck bowed low to us, but he was as solemn as an owl. He suggested all sorts of wants, some of which we could not understand in our republican simplicity, and we declined everything. He told us that the remains of Mr. Fennimore had been placed in the chapel, and that the funeral must take place the next day. Then he was considerate enough to leave us. I opened my trunk, and put on my best suit of black; but when I found that Larry was unable to make any change in his wardrobe, I resumed my travelling suit. My friend, however, looked very well, but he was certainly in no condition to attend a funeral. We were dressed just in time for dinner. A chaplain said grace at the table, and the affair was very formal to me. Little was said, and everybody seemed to be in sympathy with poor Blanche. More than once I saw the baronet gazing earnestly at Larry, who sat opposite me; and he, in his turn, looked at Blanche, who was at my side, as much as politeness would justify, perhaps more.

After dinner, I suggested to Larry that we should walk down to Bloomridge, which, near the station, was densely peopled. The baronet insisted that we should take a "dog cart," and we were forced to comply. The man drove us to the station, where we found a clothing store.

"Now, Larry, you must have a full suit of black," said I.

"I can't afford it," he promptly replied.

"But here in England you would be considered as utterly wanting in respect for the living and the dead if you should appear at a funeral in that rig."

"I can't help it."

"You are just my size; let me buy a suit, and if you don't want it after the funeral, I will take it off your hands."

I carried my point. The tailor had a coat made for another person, whom he was willing to disappoint if he could sell an additional garment, which was just a fit for my friend. We could find neither pants nor vests to match it, and the tailor agreed to make new ones by ten o'clock the next day. We assented, and I paid half the price of the suit, which was three pounds, and we returned to the hall after purchasing such other articles as we needed.

"This is cutting it rather fat for a fellow like me," said Larry.

"Or me either," I replied.

"You are not exactly a vagabond, as I am. You have plenty of money."

"It is only by accident that we are here. We shall be off in a day or two."

"I don't feel in a hurry to go. In a word, I shall feel very lonely when I can see Blanche no more," said Larry, sadly.

"Has it come to that?"

"I told you I was smitten the first time I saw her. 'Pon my word, I think she is an angel."

We talked of this matter for half an hour, and were then invited to the drawing-room. Blanche was there for a short time, but it was a very solemn assembly, and we retired early. Punctually at the appointed hour, the black suit came from the tailor's, and I paid the balance of the bill.

The funeral was to be at twelve, and we dressed for the occasion. Larry looked like another person in his sombre suit of black, with kid gloves of the same color. He seemed to have got rid of the rowdy element in his appearance, and looked like a sober and sedate young man. We attended the funeral of Mr. Fennimore, which was solemnized at a neighboring church. Though I was properly impressed by the religious services, the grief of poor Blanche was the moving element of the occasion to me. The remains of Mr. Fennimore were placed in a tomb, to be sent to America, there to be finally interred by the side of his wife. Sadly we returned to Grimsby Hall, and Sir Philip made an effort to restore some of the cheerfulness which had usually pervaded his mansion; but Blanche was hardly less gloomy than before. We spent a quiet evening in the drawing-room; but at ten o'clock the baronet desired to see Larry and myself in his library, and we promptly obeyed the summons.

CHAPTER VIII.

IN WHICH PHIL SHOWS THAT HE HAS A TALENT FOR KEEPING STILL, AND LARRY BECOMES A HERO.

THE library of the baronet's mansion was in keeping with the rest of the building, and antique carved book-cases were suitable for exhibition in the Hotel de Cluny, in Paris. The family of Sir Philip was older than the book-cases, and the talkative Breck, who did duty in our chambers as valet, so far as we were able to use the services of such a functionary, had told me that it was even more noted for its wealth than for its antiquity.

When we entered the library the baronet was walking up and down the apartment, apparently studying the figures in the carpet. I had no suspicion whatever of his object in sending for us. His manner had been somewhat strange, and I had often discovered him gazing at the face of my companion. Even in the church I had observed that he paid more attention to Larry than to the service, which certainly was not proper in a good churchman; but he was entirely excusable in the light of subsequent events. Sir Philip did not appear to notice us when we entered. A small fire of soft coal was blazing cheerfully in the grate, and his path was up and down in front of it. We walked up to a position opposite the grate, and stopped where he must pass us on his return from the farther end of the room.

"The old gentleman has something on his mind," whispered Larry.

"What can he want with us?" I asked.

"I don't know."

"I think he wants to know where you obtained his name, especially as you look so much like his grandson," I suggested.

"If he does I am in the dark on that subject. Here he comes again."

The baronet halted when he saw us, and fixed an earnest gaze on my companion.

"Young man," said he, compressing his lips after he had uttered the words, and then indulging in a long and trying pause.

"I'm at your service, sir," replied Larry, politely.

"Young man, if I should die to-night—" And then he paused again, as though he had something awfully impressive to say.

"I sincerely hope you will not die to-night, Sir Philip," added Larry. "If you do, sir, I am afraid I could not remain to attend the funeral."

"Yes, you would remain a week to attend my funeral, and not leave even after you had seen me comfortably buried."

"Perhaps I should, Sir Philip. I really hope you will live many years. You have a fine place here, and I should say that you had every means of enjoying yourself," answered my friend, with easy assurance. "I hope you will live till you are a hundred."

"Very likely you will change your mind after you know more about yourself and me," added the baronet, evidently pleased with the answers of Larry.

"I don't think so, Sir Philip. I'm a beggar myself; but I don't envy any man, woman, or child on the face of the footstool. I have as good a time as I can in the world, and I like to see other people enjoy themselves, even if they are lords, and baronets, and dukes."

"That's kind of you, and the lords, dukes, and baronets ought to be obliged to you for your consideration," added Sir Philip, chuckling at his own humor, rather than at his guest's. "Young man, if I should die to-night — " And then the baronet was very serious again, making another long pause in this place, apparently for the purpose of composing the muscles of his face.

"I am serious, Sir Philip, when I say again that I trust you will not die to-night," added Larry, who perhaps thought that the pause was intended for his benefit, and to afford him an opportunity to say something.

"Young man, if I should die to-night — "

The baronet paused again, and I observed that he was much agitated, though he labored to suppress his emotion. I elbowed Larry, and passing behind him, I told him in a whisper to say nothing; and he was silent this time. Sir Philip's lips worked as he struggled to keep down his emotion, and I thought he had some doubts as to whether or not he should utter what was upon his mind.

"Young man, if I should die to-night, in the

morning you would be Sir Lawrence Grimsby," continued the baronet, finishing the sentence this time as with a desperate effort.

As soon as he had uttered the astounding sentence, he turned and marched rapidly towards the farther end of the room.

"Here's a go!" said Larry, glancing at me, with a queer smile on his face. "The old gentleman has a weak spot in his head, or else he means to get up a thundering sensation."

"He is in earnest," I replied. "You saw his emotion."

"I did; but I'm afraid the old gentleman is crazy. Of course what he says is all bosh," laughed Larry.

"Perhaps not; let us wait and hear the conclusion of the whole matter."

My friend certainly took the astounding announcement with the utmost coolness. For my own part, I knew not what to make of it, though of course I could not help thinking of Larry's wonderful resemblance to Miles Grimsby, and the fact that he bore the family name of the baronet. Sir Philip continued to walk the room, leaving us in a very awkward and embarrassing situation, and we impatiently waited for the development of his humor. In a few moments he dropped into a large arm-chair at the side of the grate.

"Sit down," said he, pointing to a couple of chairs opposite him.

"Thank you, sir," replied Larry, as he obeyed the command, and I followed his example.

"What's your name?" demanded Sir Philip, brusquely.

"Lawrence Grimsby," replied Larry, in the same quick business tones.

"Where did you get that name?"

"I don't know, sir."

"Who are your parents?"

"I don't know, sir."

"Where were you born?"

"I don't know, sir."

"How old are you?"

"I don't know, sir."

"Do you know anything?"

"I do, sir."

"What?"

"That you are a very singular old baronet, Sir Philip."

"Good! Upon my life, you are rather more

than half right," chuckled the baronet, as he rose and rung the bell, which was instantly answered by Breck.

"Champagne," said the old gentleman, laconically, as the man appeared and disappeared almost in the same instant. "Yes, I'm a queer old fellow; but I'm not a bad man."

"You bet!"

"Sir?" interrogated the baronet, evidently unable to comprehend Larry's western Americanism.

"You remarked, Sir Philip, that you are not a bad man. You can bet on that," explained Larry; and I confess that his easy familiarity shocked and alarmed me.

"I can repeat with unction the words of the Litany, and call myself a miserable sinner, and upon my life I believe it. I have left undone those things which I ought to have done, and I have done those things which I ought not to have done," added the baronet, more seriously.

"That's just what Phil says, though not exactly in those words," added Larry, glibly.

"Pray, who's Phil?"

"Mr. Farringford here, sir. He is about the only real friend I have in the world, and he's a right down good fellow — pious, too. He has opened my eyes wider in a week than I ever could get them in my whole lifetime before."

"Never mind Phil now," said the baronet, rather petulantly.

"He is not a cipher, Sir Philip."

"I have no fault to find with him. I may say that I am very glad to find you in the company of so estimable a young gentleman; but we will speak of something else."

"I desire to be entirely ignored, sir; and if you wish, I will leave the room," I interposed.

"Not necessary, Mr. Farringford. You seem to have a talent for holding your tongue; and I have no doubt you will be able to keep to yourself whatever we wish to conceal."

"I will betray no one's confidence," I replied.

"All right, Phil; don't leave me," added Larry.

"He need not leave you, Lawrence," said Sir Philip. "Now we will attend to business."

"Precisely so, sir. You were saying — "

"Hold up! the champagne comes," interposed the old gentleman, checking Larry's remark, as Breck entered the room with a bottle and several glasses on a salver.

The well-trained servant deposited the tray on a table, and then popped the bottle of champagne. Filling three glasses, he placed them on a small salver, and passed them first to me.

"No, I thank you; none for me," I replied.

"No champagne!" exclaimed the baronet.

"No, sir; I never drink anything that can intoxicate," I replied.

"Champagne don't intoxicate, any more than goat's milk," added Sir Philip.

"Excuse me, sir; but I never drink it," I answered, embarrassed at the situation, for I knew something of the requirements of English hospitality, though I did not think they ought to compel me to make a fool or a sot of myself.

Breck presented the salver to Larry.

"I must beg to be excused, also," he replied, somewhat to my surprise.

"No champagne, Lawrence!" said Sir Philip, with a slight frown.

"None, sir; I follow Phil's lead now. At any rate, I'm going to try on his temperance principles for a while."

"Suit yourselves, young gentlemen," added the baronet, impatiently.

Breck passed the salver to him, and he took his glass. The servant then placed the table at the side of his master, on which he put the tray, with the bottle upon it, adjusting the cork, so as to prevent the effervescence as much as possible of its contents.

"Mr. Miles is in the drawing-room, sir; and the ladies have all retired," said Breck, as he finished with careful precision the arrangements which were plainly an every-day routine with him.

"Give him my good night, and bid him retire, also," replied the baronet.

Breck was evidently dissatisfied with this decision, and I concluded that Miles was in the habit of visiting the library in the later part of the evening, and probably drank champagne with his grandfather; but the man was too well trained to say anything more, and retired at once.

"If I should die to-night, you would be Sir Lawrence Grimsby in the morning," said the baronet again, as he drained his glass. "Now I dare say you are willing I should finish this bottle alone, and even send for another, for with your tee-total principles, you believe it will help me off."

"If I knew I should attain to the distinguished

position you suggest, Sir Philip, I should still ask my friend Phil to pray that you might live to be eighty, at least; I don't pray myself."

"I don't believe it, you rascal! When you know me more, you will love me less."

"I hope not, Sir Philip; but of course I can't tell," answered Larry, with refreshing candor.

"No, you don't hope not," added the baronet, as he filled and drank off another glass of champagne.

"I'm bound to say I shouldn't love a man if he wasn't a good fellow, even though he was a baronet. A man might be a baronet and still be a rascal; but I don't believe you are anything of the sort."

"Upon my life, I believe I am!"

"Upon my soul, I believe you are not."

"Don't be so rude, Larry," I said in a whisper.

"Let him speak his mind, Mr. Farringford; I like it," interposed Sir Philip; and I subsided at once.

"I can't very well help saying just what I think," continued Larry.

"Good! I knew another young fellow who was just as blunt and independent," replied Sir Philip, with more emotion than I could explain.

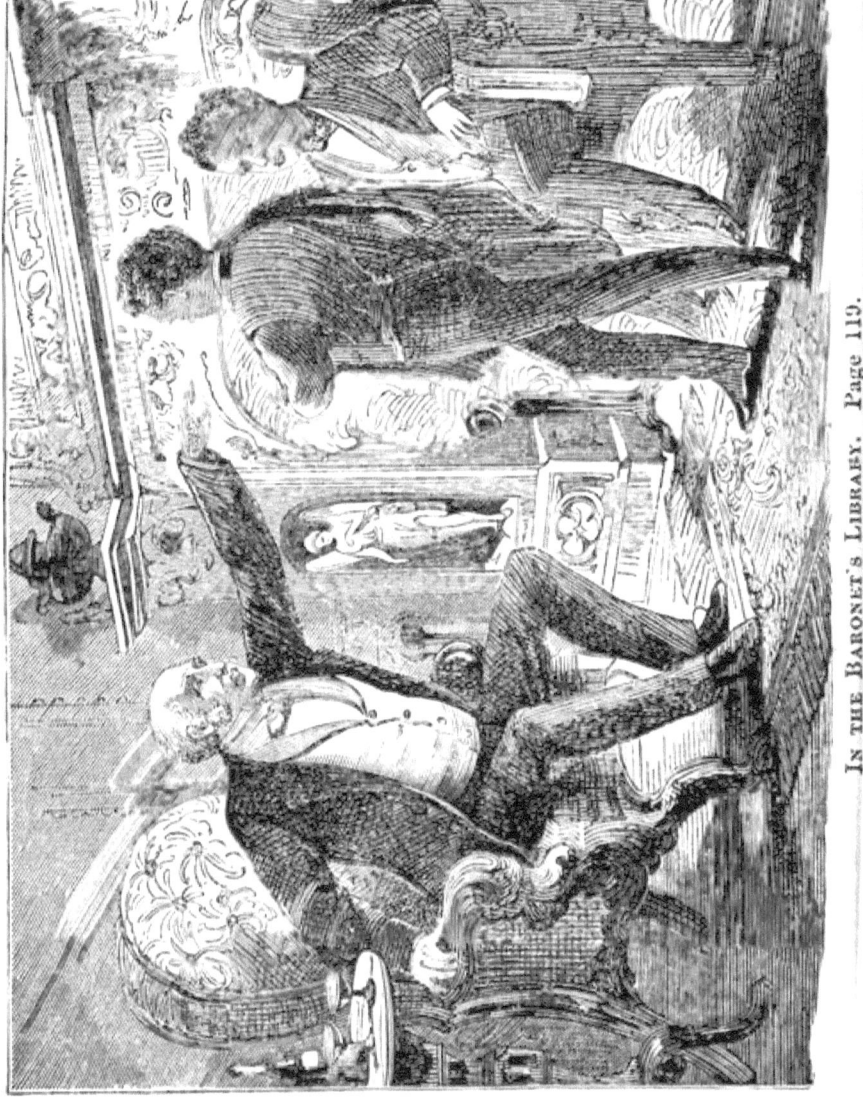

IN THE BARONET'S LIBRARY. Page 119.

"Who was he, sir?" asked Larry.

"Take off your coat, Lawrence," said the old gentleman, sharply.

My friend promptly sprang to his feet at this singular command, but paused, and glanced at the baronet, as if to ascertain whether he was in earnest.

"Off with it," said the baronet, making a gesture of impatience.

Larry quickly took off his black coat, and tossed it into his chair.

"Roll up your shirt-sleeve on the left arm," continued Sir Philip, much excited, as he rose from his chair.

Larry complied.

"Turn round to the light. There it is!"

The baronet dropped back into his chair.

"What is it?" asked Larry. "Do you mean my raspberry?"

"The red mark on your left arm. It is about the size and color of a red raspberry," replied the old gentleman, struggling to be calm, and succeeding tolerably well. "Did you ever see it before, Lawrence?"

"To be sure I have. I remember that mark as long as I can remember anything."

"Let me see it again," added Sir Philip, rising and taking a musty letter from the writing-table. "I can't see; read, Mr. Farringford, from the top of the third page."

"'The vaccination mark is one inch lower, and half an inch nearer the body, than the reddish spot, which is shaped like a raspberry. I know no —'"

"That's enough. Let us see if it is so."

Both of us compared the marks with the description.

"The measurements are not right; but the child has become a man, and they would not remain the same," said Sir Philip.

"The relative positions are as described in the letter," I added.

"Precisely; there is no doubt of it; but the name and the boy's features are enough. I am satisfied. Lawrence, you are my grandson, beyond the possibility of a doubt. Put on your coat."

"I am very glad to be anybody's grandson, more especially yours, Sir Philip," answered Larry, who was not half so much excited by the remarkable events of the evening as I was. "I have been a waif all my life, and it is rather jolly to think of being picked up by a grandfather; but

I'm afraid there's some mistake. Somebody has been getting up a cheap romance at my expense. I don't want to be a hero. I hate the very idea."

" Keep quiet, my boy."

" Don't attempt to hug me, or anything of that sort. If you do, I shall scream like a heroine."

" Don't disturb yourself; I shall not hug you yet; but a mistake is utterly impossible," added the baronet, and he quaffed another glass of wine. " I will explain it all now."

But at that moment there was a knock at the door, and Miles Grimsby entered when his grandfather told him to " come in."

CHAPTER IX.

IN WHICH PHIL RELATES THE STORY THE BARONET TOLD, AND LARRY MEETS BLANCHE IN THE GARDEN.

"WELL, Miles, what do you want? Didn't I send word to you that you might retire?" said the baronet, when his grandson entered the library.

"You did, sir; but it is very unusual for you to send me to bed without bidding me good night; and now I have been absent half a year," replied Miles, glancing first at Larry and then at me, as though he feared some conspiracy against him was in progress.

"You are quite right, Miles, my boy. There; give me your hand, boy; good night, and God bless you!"

"Good night, grandfather," replied the young man; but he did not seem disposed to go.

The baronet was silent then, and Miles, finding

that his presence was a burden, left the room; but I saw the flush of anger on his cheek, and he slammed the door behind him more violently than the occasion required.

"Poor fellow! I'm sorry for him," said Sir Philip; "but I must do justice, tardy though it be, before God and man. I think the boy suspects something."

"I have no desire to injure Miles, Sir Philip," protested Larry.

"I dare say you have not, Lawrence; but you have put the boy's nose out of joint: you have, indeed, and his father's, too. As I said before, if I should die to-night, you would be Sir Lawrence Grimsby in the morning. I will tell you all about it now, and to-morrow I shall go with you before a magistrate, and acknowledge you as my grandson."

I will give Sir Philip's story in substance, for he elaborated the details much more than is necessary for my present purpose. The baronet was now sixty-six years old, but he appeared to be entirely hale and hearty, though I fancied that he would go off suddenly before many years, if he drank as much wine every night as on the present occasion. He had been the father of three sons, the oldest of whom, Philip, was of course the heir to the baronet's title and estates. The name of the second son was Lawrence, while the third was Miles, the only one at present living. Twenty years before, Lawrence had married a poor girl, whose only dowry was her beauty. Sir Philip was violently opposed to this match; for the girl was not only penniless, but was the daughter of a poor mechanic. He assured his son he would disown and cast him out if he persisted in his disobedience; but Lawrence was an independent young man, and was, withal, so deeply smitten with the low-born maiden that he persisted in his purpose, and married her. The baronet was true to his promise. He disowned and cast off the disobedient son, refusing even to see him, or to grant him a penny to supply his wants.

Lawrence had been brought up to no occupation, and he could do nothing in England, though he remained there until after the birth of his only child. He borrowed money enough to convey his little family to New York. He was determined to struggle manfully with his hard lot; but he had no qualifications for business, and the battle went against him. He obtained a small situation as a clerk, but was unable even to retain this, and actually suffered for the want of food. For the want of the comforts of life his wife died. Then he wrote to his father; but the baronet sternly refused to heed the touching appeal. Lawrence struggled only for a brief period more with the rough fortunes of life, and then died himself, and was buried by public charity. While he was sick, and only waiting for death to put an end to his misery, he wrote again to his father, appealing to him this time only for the little child, which had already been sent to the Orphan Asylum. He described the boy, so that his father's agent might identify him, and was careful that he should bear his own name.

This letter touched the heart of Sir Philip, and he privately sent an agent to look up the father and the child. The former was dead and in his grave, and the agent was unable to find the latter. In the mean time another grief had come to soften the heart of the baronet. His oldest son was killed by a fall from his horse in a fox hunt. Philip, this son, had died unmarried, though he was engaged to the daughter of a peer at the time of the fatal accident. A second attempt was made to find the son of Lawrence, but without any better success. Miles, the third son, had married a daughter of Sir Hale Groveland, Knight, and was the father of several children, of whom Miles was the oldest, and at the death of his father would have been the heir of the title and estates, if my friend Larry had not stepped between him and his apparent destiny. Mr. Fennimore had married another daughter of Sir Hale Groveland, which explained the connection between the families.

"Do you understand it now, Lawrence?" asked the baronet, as he finished his recital.

"Perfectly, sir; the matter is double leaded, with a pica fist before it. Your first son, Philip, who was the heir of the title and its appendages, is dead. My father came next," replied Larry.

"Yes, my boy; for Philip died without issue. Then, as your father is dead, you come next."

"Just so; and Miles is left out in the cold."

"Of course I shall take care of him and his father, in my will; but the bulk of my property goes to you, Lawrence."

"Well, sir, I hope you will not have occasion to part with it for a good many years. But I desire to make an even thing of it."

"Impossible!" exclaimed the baronet.

"As for the title, Miles senior and his son may have that. I wouldn't turn my hand for it," added Larry, with easy indifference.

"It can't be done. These things are all fixed by the laws and customs of England, and must not be set aside. It is a new matter to you now, and you will change your mind in regard to the title in a few months, or weeks."

"Perhaps I shall."

"If I live till to-morrow, I shall arrange everything. In the mean time, not a word must be said about this business. I don't wish to stir up my son and grandson yet; and I want time to look the matter over. Now you may retire, my boys."

"I was going to London, to-morrow, with Phil," said Larry.

"Go with him, if you like. I would rather have you out of the way for a few weeks."

"Right, Sir Philip. I would like to take a run on the continent, and see a little of the world there, but I don't happen to have the needful."

"Do you mean money?"

"That's exactly what I mean; and that has been the one thing needful to me all my life."

"You shall not want for money, if fifty thousand pounds will supply your needs."

"I don't want fifty thousand pounds; only — let me see — eleven or twelve thousand, at present," replied Larry, lightly.

"You shall have it to-morrow morning, if you desire."

"I do desire it very much indeed. Ten thousand pounds would do me more good than anything else in the world. I would rather have it than be an earl or a duke."

"You shall have it; though it is rather a large sum for a boy; but I am willing to make up for the past with you. Now, go to your rooms. I am tired."

We went to our chambers. I was amazed at the coolness and self-possession of my friend. I was excited myself, but he was not.

"You are the strangest mortal I ever saw, Larry!" I exclaimed, as we dismissed the valet, and I closed the door behind him.

"I know it," replied he, with a light laugh. "'Pon my word, you speak only the truth, as you always do, Phil."

"You don't seem to be the least moved or excited at your remarkably good fortune."

"The fact is, Phil, I have always had a feeling that I was born for something of this kind, and I am not much surprised at what has occurred."

"I am. Yesterday you were a vagabond; to-day, the heir of one of the richest houses in England."

"I shall be able to pay you the little sum I borrowed of you now, Phil."

"Never mind that. I think you are a modest young man, Larry, most astoundingly so. What in the world did you mean by asking Sir Philip for eleven or twelve thousand pounds."

"I have a pressing need for that little sum."

"Are you mad? Do you know how much you asked for?"

"I think I do — eleven or twelve thousand pounds."

"Between fifty and sixty thousand dollars!"

"Just so; I had arithmetic enough to figure that out."

"But you cannot mean it."

"'Pon my word I do — every penny of it."

"No, you don't; you can't use it. Two or three thousand dollars is all you need to spend on the continent, even if you travel like a prince."

"I don't want it for that. I want ten thousand of it for quite another purpose. Draw near to me, Phil; open your ears, and listen to me. 'He that hath ears to hear, let him hear.' I set that up once, as the text of a sermon, which explains how I happen to remember it. Do you know Miss Blanche Fennimore?"

"Of course I do."

"So do I. Possibly you may know that her father got into some sort of difficulty with the bank at Lowerville," continued Larry, very seriously.

"Certainly I do; you are aware that I am in possession of all the facts," I answered, impatiently.

"Probably Blanche has no suspicion that her father was anything but an honest, upright man."

"We are certain that she knows nothing about the crime of her father."

"According to your Christian logic, Phil, the first thing a man should do to atone for his crime is to make all the reparation in his power."

"To be sure; and Mr. Fennimore did all that was in his power."

"Well, I propose to do what it was not in his

power to do; in other words, to make good the rest of his defalcation. How is that for high?"

"Why should you do such a thing?" I asked, amazed at this proposition.

"Not for my own sake, I grant, but for Blanche's. If she should ever learn that her father's fingers were greasy in the money-bags, don't you think she would feel better about it if she knew that every red had been restored to the bank?"

"Certainly she would; but I do not see that you are called upon to do such a romantic deed," I replied.

"Romantic — is it?" laughed Larry. "Well, perhaps it is. Who knows? I'm not much on romance; but if the baronet ponies up the rocks, I shall pay every red that Blanche's father stole or owed. Phil, I love that girl."

"You are smitten, I know; but don't hurry about the matter."

"Hurry? I'm up to my ears now. You might as well attempt to check Niagara as a thing of this kind. I've got it bad, Phil."

"I'm sorry for you, Larry."

"You needn't be. I'm no longer a vagabond,

and the case looks hopeful to me now, though it never did before."

"You are getting tame and commonplace now, and I think we had better turn in."

It seemed incredible to me, but Larry was snoring in ten minutes more; yet I must do him the justice to say that he snored only when he was very tired. He had slept very little during the voyage, and neither the thought of Blanche, nor of the good fortune that had so suddenly overtaken him, could keep him awake. I agreed with him in considering his case a very hopeful one; for the heart of the fair girl was filled with gratitude to him for his care of her father. Of course she had not thought of love; but she was kindly disposed towards him.

We did not get up very early the next morning. Attached to the Hall was a beautiful garden, in which Larry and I walked before breakfast. On a rustic bridge across the brook that wandered through the garden we met Blanche. She was very sad; but she smiled when she saw us, and extended her hand to both.

"I suppose we must leave you to-day, Miss Fennimore," said Larry, as we walked along together.

The Meeting in the Garden. Page 132.

"So soon?"

"We have already staid longer than we intended," I added. "Perhaps we may never see you again."

"Do not say that; I am sure I should be very unhappy if I believed I were never again to see such good friends as you have been to me — and my father," she answered, with much emotion. "Do come to Grimsby Hall when you return from the continent; for I am to stay with my aunt this summer, and perhaps longer."

"I shall certainly come again, whether Mr. Farringford does or not," said Larry.

"I shall be so glad to see you! But I hope you will both come. I shall be so lonely, now that he is gone!" she replied, her voice choking as she thought of her father. "I shall never think of him without thinking of you."

"If I never see you again, I never shall forget you," continued Larry; and after this remark, I thought I had better drop a reasonable distance behind them, though I knew that my friend had too much good sense to make a "declaration" at such a time, and under such circumstances.

My plan was assisted by Miles, who presently joined me from a by-path. I saw that he was troubled, but I hoped he would not speak to me about our conference with Sir Philip.

"I hear you are off to-day, Phil," said he.

"Yes, we go to London by the noon train."

"And where then are you going?"

"I go to Nice, by the way of Paris and Marseilles."

"But there is going to be a bloody big row in Italy this summer."

"For that reason I am in haste to find my mother before the war breaks up the travel."

"Perhaps you won't mind telling me what you were talking about with Sir Philip last night," said he, after a short pause.

"I would rather Sir Philip should tell you himself, if he thinks proper," I replied.

"You won't tell me, then?"

"I do not feel at liberty to do so without your grandfather's permission."

"You needn't trouble yourself. I know now."

"Indeed?"

"I do, indeed."

"The matter does not concern me, and I have nothing to say or do about it."

"By the noon train," said he. "I am going up to London at the same time."

"We should be happy to have your company."

"Thanks;" and without another word he turned into a side-path, and disappeared.

His conduct appeared very singular to me.

CHAPTER X.

IN WHICH PHIL AND LARRY GO TO LONDON, AND MILES GRIMSBY IS VERY MUCH EXCITED.

THE actions of Miles Grimsby were not easy to explain. He told me bluntly that he knew the subject of the conversation with the baronet in the library; but I did not see how this was possible, even if he had so far lost his self-respect as to become an eavesdropper; for the fireplace, near which we sat, was too far from the door to permit a listener to hear what was said. Of course he knew the story of his uncle Lawrence, and I concluded that he simply suspected the relation of my friend to him. I did not see Larry again till we met at the breakfast table. Whatever the nature of the interview between him and Miss Fennimore, there was nothing in her look to indicate that anything unusual had occurred, though I did think my friend was more cheerful.

After the meal, we went with the baronet to a magistrate, a gentleman of distinction, and, I at once inferred, an intimate friend of Sir Philip.

"Here he is, Sir John," said the baronet, indicating Larry with a nod of his head.

"Impossible!" exclaimed the magistrate, with a promptness which showed that this was not the first time the subject had been mentioned. "You are deceived."

"No, I am not. I purpose to prove all I say, inch by inch, to your satisfaction, Sir John; and mulish as you are, you will be satisfied before I am done. I have no time to spare, and we will begin at once."

Sir Philip placed the letters of his deceased son in the hands of the magistrate.

"You have read them before," he continued. "Off with your coat, Lawrence."

Larry prepared himself for this examination. While he was doing so, Sir Philip produced a miniature of his deceased son Lawrence. It was painted on ivory; and looking at the face alone, I should have supposed it to be the portrait of Larry. Sir John acknowledged that the picture was a perfect likeness. The blood mark on the arm corresponded with the description in the letter, and after Larry had related all that he knew, or had heard, of his early life, the magistrate declared that he was satisfied. He wrote a document, which covered a page of foolscap, to the effect that Sir Philip acknowledged Larry to be the son of his deceased son Lawrence, which we all signed, and the business was finished. From the magistrate's we went to the banker's, where the baronet drew twelve thousand pounds, in Bank of England notes.

"Here, my boy," said Sir Philip, as he handed him the entire amount.

"But, Sir Philip, I intended to tell you what I wished to do with this money," replied Larry, as he coolly took the roll of bills. "Perhaps you will not approve the purpose to which I shall apply it."

"Don't tell me anything about it. I am too nervous to hear. I regard this money as a small drop of atonement for the past. Say nothing more about it."

"I shall send most of it to America."

"Send it to China, if you like. Have you seen Miles to-day?"

"Yes, sir, I saw him, but did not speak with him."

"I met him in the garden," I interposed, and related what had passed between him and myself.

"The boy understands it all," said the baronet, uneasily. "He is a strange fellow; but I don't know that there is anything bad about him. Did he say he was going to London by the noon train?"

"He did, sir."

"He always has his own way. He has been a pet at Grimsby Hall. Let him go to London, if he pleases. Very likely he wishes to consult some lawyer there. It would not be strange if I outlived the boy's father, who is feeble in body and mind."

I had already concluded that all was not right with the elder Miles. He seldom spoke to any one, and had a vacant expression. Though his wife had been absent six months, I observed that he had little or nothing to say to her. On the whole, it seemed to me like a very strange family.

We saw Blanche again, and I was satisfied that an excellent understanding subsisted between her and Larry. Each promised to write the other. My friend had also agreed to write to his grandfather every week. A carriage conveyed us to the station, and we were attended by the baronet and Blanche; but Miles went in the dog cart by himself.

"Now, good by, my boy," said Sir Philip. "Take good care of yourself; for I depend more on you than on any one else. When I write to you to come home, come without an hour's delay."

"I will obey you in all things, sir," replied Larry.

"Are you going to London, Miles?" asked the baronet, as the young man stepped up to him.

"Yes, sir; I want to see some American friends there. I may go over the continent with them."

"Have you money enough?"

"Plenty, sir."

"God bless you, my boy. Take care of yourself," added the baronet, but with less feeling, I thought, than he had spoken to Larry.

Though the intercourse between Miles and his grandfather was attended with all the forms of love and tenderness, I began to see that it was rather formal. We stepped into an empty compartment, as the train stopped, and were soon on our way to London. Miles placed himself at the farther end of the compartment, and did not speak for an hour. His presence prevented Larry and myself from talking of what was uppermost in our minds; but for my own part, I was content to gaze on the bright green fields of England, and see what I could of the beautiful country. Miles was very nervous and uneasy, fidgeting from one seat to another, trying to look out at the open window, but occasionally casting furtive glances at Larry and me. When he had kept this up until the train was half way to London, he came to our end of the compartment, and seated himself at my side, facing my friend. It was evident that he intended to say something, but he only looked at Larry for several minutes.

"It seems that you don't look like me for nothing," said he, at last.

"Well, Miles, I don't think I look any more like you than you do like me," replied Larry, smiling. "I don't know whether you mean to say that John Jones looks like the king, or the king like John Jones."

"Either way you please. I only meant to say that there is a strong resemblance between us."

"Right; I grant that."

"It is not accidental," added Miles, nervously.

"I'm no philosopher."

"What were you and my grandfather talking about last night?"

"For further particulars, apply to Sir Philip Grimsby, Bart., Grimsby Hall," laughed Larry.

"Well, I know."

"If you do, it is folly to ask."

"You are the son of my uncle Lawrence, who died in America."

"Is that so?" demanded Larry.

"You know that it is."

"Cousin, your hand, if that is so; and thank you for the information," replied Larry, extending his hand to the discomfited young man. "If what you say is true, we are cousins."

"We are," answered Miles, taking the offered hand. "But I'm not glad to see you."

"That's candid and honest; but are you quite sure that what you say is true?"

"Why did my grandfather send for you last night? Why did you stay with him till morning? Where did you go with him this forenoon?"

"Ask Sir Philip."

"I have no occasion to ask him."

"Have you taken the dimensions of the keyhole of Sir Philip's library door?"

"No! Don't insult me!"

"I will not; pardon me."

"Since you have uttered a suspicion, I will say that I did not hear a word that was said in the library, or anywhere else, on this subject, between you and my grandfather; but I understand it all. My mother gave me all the information I needed."

"Miles, I haven't a word to say about it," added Larry, more earnestly than he had yet spoken.

"I took you for a good fellow on board of the steamer, and I expected something like magnanimity from you," muttered Miles.

"Magnanimity is a long word, and I am not in a condition to be magnanimous towards you. If the time ever comes when I can exercise this noble sentiment in regard to you, I trust I shall not be found wanting."

"That won't do," growled Miles.

"But it must do," answered Larry, with energy.

"Don't make me your enemy, Lawrence."

"I don't intend to do that; but if you insist

upon being my enemy, I suppose I must submit, for I can't help myself."

"I give you fair and timely warning," added Miles, shaking his head.

"I acknowledge the receipt of the fair and timely warning," said Larry, with the most provoking indifference.

"What do you desire of Larry?" I asked, fearful that a quarrel was brewing, and desirous of avoiding any unpleasantness.

"I desire him to be candid and honest with me, which he will not. He pretends to know nothing about the matter of which I speak. He will neither deny nor acknowledge the truth of what I say," replied Miles, turning to me, much excited.

"I have been present at all the interviews of my friend with Sir Philip, and what passed between them was entirely confidential. The baronet imposed silence upon Larry and upon me, and without acknowledging or denying the truth of what you say, Miles, neither he nor I have any right to repeat a word that passed at these conferences. Larry is entirely honorable about the matter, and no gentleman should attempt to worm out of another what the latter distinctly declares is confidential."

"Do you mean to tell me that I am no gentleman?" demanded Miles, whose tone and manner indicated that I had not bettered the matter.

"Nothing of the kind; but I trust you will see that it is not proper to press this subject any farther;" I promptly replied.

"But the subject concerns me more nearly than any other person, and is of vastly more consequence to me than to my father, or even my grandfather. If Larry comes to England and to Grimsby Hall as the son of my uncle Lawrence, he robs me of my inheritance, and makes a beggar of me. Do you expect me to keep quiet under such circumstances?" continued Miles, warming up at what he evidently regarded as his wrongs.

"The statement you make is neither admitted nor denied, and we can say nothing about the matter."

"That will do, Phil. Don't open your mouth on the subject again."

"Your friend is an adventurer," added Miles, still addressing me. "I was till yesterday the prospective heir of the title and estates of my grandfather. Now he steps in between me and all my earthly hopes."

"This is a fine country, Phil," said Larry.

"And he refuses me even a word of explanation," persisted Miles.

"Beautiful country," I added.

"Sir Philip is one of the ten richest men in England, and his estates and income would all have been mine, if your friend had not come here to blast my hopes."

"That's a pretty stream of water; I suppose they call it a river over here," said Larry.

"Very likely; there isn't room enough here for such rivers as the Mississippi, the Ohio, or even the Hudson."

"You do not hear what I say," interposed Miles.

"Every word of it; but we respectfully decline to continue the conversation on the subject you have chosen, for the reason we have distinctly stated," I replied, gently, but firmly.

"I see that you intend to add insult to injury," muttered Miles.

"Far from it."

"I give you fair warning, Lawrence Grimsby, if that be your name, which I doubt."

"Receipt of warning duly acknowledged, Miles Grimsby, if that is your name, which I don't doubt; and I will give it to you in writing if you desire," replied Larry.

"You have made me your enemy."

"Sorry for it, but must submit."

Miles suddenly darted to the corner of the compartment which he had before occupied, and, very much agitated, drummed on the floor with his feet, and pounded the cushions with his hands. I was sorry for him, though, if my friend was really the son of Lawrence Grimsby, deceased, Miles had no right to complain. Certainly Larry had done nothing himself to provoke the disappointed young man; on the contrary, he had been very forbearing under his charges. During the rest of the journey Miles twice attempted to resume the subject; but we declined even to speak of it again. When the train stopped at Euston Square station, in London, he darted out of the carriage with his portmanteau in his hand, and disappeared in the crowd. Larry and I took a cab, and drove to Morley's, in Trafalgar Square. We took a room together.

"Phil, this money is heavy in my pocket, and it must be started off at once," said Larry.

"Are you determined to do this romantic act, Larry?" I asked.

"Undoubtedly I am. I haven't wavered or hesitated the millionth part of a second in my purpose. You have the address of the president of that bank in Lowerville. Now write a letter to him; tell him to put this money into his bank, and never open his head to a single soul on earth, except to say that Mr. Fennimore's estate don't owe the concern a red cent. I shall not feel easy till the money is on its way."

I wrote the letter as Larry dictated, and then we went to my bankers'. A bill on New York, in favor of the president of the bank, was purchased, the duplicates to be forwarded by the bankers which I enclosed in the letter I had written. I requested the gentleman to address his reply to "Lawrence Grimsby, Esq.," care of my bankers. My friend then invested the greater part of his remaining funds in a letter of credit, good anywhere in Europe.

"Now I feel more like a Christian than I ever did before in the whole course of my life," said Larry, as we left the bankers'. "I even feel like forgiving grandfather Sir Philip for making me a rich man."

"I dare say you do. But how in regard to Miles?"

"I don't feel a bit hard towards him. I'm sorry for him: if I were he, perhaps I should be as much disgruntled as he is; but I doubt it. Now, Phil, let me pay you what I owe you; for really that's one of the greatest pleasures in the known world."

Larry paid me the money I had advanced in cash and for clothing; but I positively refused to take the sum I had given after the accident, and we compromised it by his purchashing a gold watch at Bennett's, on the case of which he had my name engraved as the giver.

CHAPTER XI.

IN WHICH PHIL AND LARRY MAKE THE ACQUAINTANCE OF A MAN WITH A PREPOSTEROUS HAT, AND START FOR ITALY.

I COULD not lose sight of the fact that I was in London, the metropolis of the world, though I had not time to see its sights. I was deeply interested in its crowded streets and its massive public buildings. From the bankers' we went down to London Bridge, then to the Bank, the Tower of London, and other sights in that part of the city. The next day we went to Westminster Abbey and Palace, through the Parks, and into the British Museum. This was all we were able to see of London on this visit. I had stopped longer than I intended already, and I was in haste to reach Paris, where I expected to find a letter from Marian Collingsby, my cousin, who had promised to give me the latest intelligence in regard to **my** mother.

On the morning of the third day after our arrival, we left for Paris, and arrived in the evening of the same day. I hastened to the bankers, and found three letters, one from Marian, one from Ella Gracewood, and one from my father. My cousin informed me that my mother had gone to Milan, to spend several weeks with some Italian friends, whose address she was unable to give me. My father assured me that he was still well and happy, and Ella's letter gave me a fluttering of the heart, though it contained nothing which need be transcribed to these pages. It was a very pleasant letter, and one of that kind which a young man reads all the way from twenty to a hundred times.

Larry and I walked about the city for two hours, till we had a tolerable idea of the central portion, and then returned to the Hotel Meurice, where we had taken a double room. The city was in a blaze of excitement over the Italian war. The emperor and the army had gone to take part in the conflict which was to end in the expulsion of the Austrians from Lombardy. The enthusiasm was tremendous, and Larry and myself were infected with it; for it seemed to us like a war for liberty. Then France appeared to represent the highest ideal of justice, and to bear a chivalrous part in redeeming the oppressed from the oppressor. Garibaldi's name was on every lip, and the famous hymn that bears his name was played by every band, and whistled and sung by all the people.

"There will be a lively time in Italy when we get there, Phil," said Larry.

"I think so; and I am afraid the war will spoil all my calculations," I replied, as we entered the garden of the Tuileries, where a band of music had attracted a great crowd.

"This music stirs me clear down to my boots. I believe, if I knew French well enough, I should enter the army as a volunteer."

"You don't mean it."

"Yes, I do. I never cared much about playing soldier; but when it comes to the real matter, I believe in it."

"But you have no wish to take part in these European quarrels."

"Why not? I believe in liberty. Austria and tyranny mean the same thing."

"Your circumstances have changed."

"They have; but I have not changed. I am the same old sixpence. I wish I could talk French."

"You say you can read it a little."

"I can; but I can't tell what one of these Frenchmen says when he speaks any more than if he spoke the Hottentot lingo. You seem to be quite at home at it, Phil."

"I began to study French when I was ten years old, and have kept it up ever since. Miss Gracewood and I used to practise every day. I find I can get along very well."

"First rate. By the way, Phil, do you see that long-haired fellow on your right, smoking a cigar?" said Larry, nodding towards the individual.

"Yes; and I have seen him half a dozen times before to-day, in the steamer and on the train from London."

The man to whom Larry alluded had long, black hair, and a long, black mustache. He wore a rather threadbare suit of black, with a black hat which had possibly been in fashion some time during the last ten years; for it was preposterously high in the crown and narrow in the brim. I had heard and read a great deal about the spy system of Paris, and I could not help connecting this man with the French "shadows," who worm themselves into the confidence of all sorts of people, and worm out of them all sorts of secrets. He looked like a tricky and cunning man; but as he had come from London with us, a second thought assured me that my suspicion was absurd. While I was thinking of the matter I saw four policemen approaching us. I had seen some of these *sergents de ville* near the station, and many of them in the streets and boulevards. I could not help admiring their dress and bearing. They wore gray linen pants, and dark-blue dress coats, having rather long and broad skirts, buttoned up to the throat, janty chapeaux on their heads, and a light, slender sword at the side, which hung from a belt inside of the coat. I looked at them again, and more than ever admired their appearance. They walked directly towards us, and I was about to express my favorable opinion of them to my friend, when, to my utter astonishment, two of them "surrounded" me, and the other two performed a similar service for Larry.

"*Pardon, monsieur*," said one of the pair at my side, as they locked their arms in mine, and began to move me towards the Rue Rivoli.

"*Qu'est ce que vous voulez?*" I demanded.

"*Pardon, monsieur,*" was the only reply I received, as the men hurried me over the walks towards the street.

"I say, Phil, how's this?" called Larry.

"I don't know; I don't understand it."

"*Vous vous trompez!*" (you are mistaken), exclaimed some one in a new voice behind me.

The policemen halted, and suddenly released their hold of Larry and myself. Turning to see who had thus kindly interposed in our favor, I discovered the seedy, long-haired individual.

"*Les messieurs sont Américains,*" added he, shaking his head vigorously, as though he was much mortified at the blunder.

"*Pardon, messieurs,*" said the officers, as they politely touched their chapeaux, and walked away into the crowd.

What had passed satisfied me in regard to the long-haired individual, that he was a member of the secret police, a spy, or a stool-pigeon. He took off his preposterous hat, bowed low, demanded "*pardon,*" and hastily retreated towards the Rue Rivoli; for the crowd, never partial to men of his cloth, were looking at him with suspicion and disfavor.

"I am sorry it ended so abruptly," laughed Larry. "I wanted to see more of it; for I was in hopes we were arrested as red republicans, or something of that sort, and I rather like an adventure."

"I am not at all anxious to be detained a week or more here, though I suppose my passport would have got me out of the scrape. By the way, Larry, you ought to have such a document."

"I wouldn't give two cents for a barrel of them. What do I want of a passport?"

"To prove that you are an American citizen."

"If Sir Philip Grimsby and the spot on my arm don't lie, I'm not an American citizen."

"No; you are a Briton."

"I don't half like the idea; but the pile of money has a reconciling influence."

When the band in the garden had finished the concert, we went over to the Hotel Meurice. As we entered the court-yard, we saw the long-haired individual seated in one of the iron chairs, quietly smoking a cheap cigar, as I judged it was by the villanous odor it exhaled. As soon as he perceived us, he sprang to his feet, hastily removed his preposterous hat, and bowed with the most extravagant deference.

"How are you, old boy? What's the meaning of the farce you played off on us in the garden?" said Larry, not supposing that the long-haired gentleman could speak English.

"I came here to beg your pardon for the mistake," replied he, bowing low again.

"Ah, Mr. Jones, you speak English!"

"O, yes; I speak English, French, German, Spanish, Portuguese, and Italian, which is my native language."

"Bully for you!" exclaimed Larry. "Of course, with as many lingos as that, you don't know how to hold your tongue."

"Even better than I do to speak," replied he, blandly.

"What did you take us to be?" I inquired.

"I took you to be American gentlemen. I made no mistake. It was the stupid policemen."

"Whom were you looking for?"

"For London pickpockets: two came in the train to-day."

"Then you are a police spy, Mr. Jones?" inquired Larry.

"Do not mention it, if you please. I interfered and betrayed myself rather than permit the police to annoy you, even for a moment."

"All right, Mr. Jones. That was doing the handsome thing, Mr. Jones."

"My name is Cuore [Koo-ó-ray] — Giovanni Cuore, at your service," added the spy, bowing again. "In English, you would call me John Hart."

"How did you know that we were Americans?" I asked.

"I heard you speak of America on the steamer. I shall have the two pickpockets arrested, and then I shall go to Italy," continued Cuore, who seemed to be very communicative for a man whose business it was to keep still. "I shall go to Nizza [Neet-za] to-morrow night."

"Where is Nizza?" I inquired.

"Ah, in English you call it Nice [Nees], as in French."

"Are you going to Nice?" And I was much interested then, for I intended to go there myself, in order to obtain some information in regard to my mother.

"Yes; to Nice, and then to Milan, where I was born, and lived till I was twenty-two."

This was exactly my own route, and I at once regarded Signor Cuore as a person I wished to know better.

"But the Austrians will not allow you to visit Milan," I suggested.

"I go where I please, in spite of Austrians, French, or Sardinians," he replied, significantly.

"I suppose you intend to go into the spy business," I added.

"Possibly," said he, shrugging his shoulders. "But I must look for the two pickpockets. I know where to find them, and in another hour they will be in the *Conciergerie*. I only came to apologize for the mistake;" and taking off his hat, he began to retreat backward towards the entrance.

"One moment, Monsieur Cuore. Will you breakfast with us to-morrow morning at nine?" I interposed.

"You do me very great honor," he replied, with the same extravagant deference.

"But I desire very much to see you again."

"I will accept your considerate invitation with great pleasure."

"Nine o'clock."

"Nine o'clock; *bon soir, monsieur*," he answered, and departed.

"What do you want of that cove, Phil?" demanded Larry.

"He is going to Italy, and is an Italian. He can help me."

"How do you know but he is a government spy?"

"I don't care if he is. I have no intention of subverting the government, or taking part with the Austrians: so I have nothing to fear from all the spies in the world."

We walked about the city during the evening, and retired early. The next day all Paris was ringing with the news of the battle of Montebello, in which the French and Sardinians defeated the Austrians. Punctually at nine o'clock came Signor Cuore. He assured us the London pickpockets were arrested, and that his mission was ended. He made himself very agreeable, and was satisfied that I should be able to enter Milan, if I would submit to his direction. He would aid me in every possible way. Indeed, Signor Cuore seemed to exist just then for the sole purpose of serving me.

"We must go to Marseilles, and then by steamer to Nice. The train leaves the station Boulevard Mazas at twenty minutes past eight this evening," said Cuore, as he bowed and scraped his adieus.

"Now, Larry, I don't wish to drag you after me," said I, when the spy had gone.

"Wherever thou goest, I goest," laughed he.

"I am going into a disturbed country."

"So much the better. If I can get near enough to a great battle to see it, I shall do so. As I told you, I had just as lief live as die, and I should really like to take a hand in the fight for United Italy. I hate an Austrian as bad as any of them."

"I may get near enough to be in danger. I shall heed no peril. If I am sure that my mother is in Milan, I shall go there at all hazards; for she may need my assistance, and one don't know what may happen in war. But I won't ask you to go into danger."

"I don't care for danger, Phil. I'm not a chicken, and I think I can stand it anywhere you can."

"I have been under fire, you know; in fact, in a battle."

"In a little Indian squabble," laughed Larry. "I have been in a street fight, which is about the same thing."

"I think not; about twenty men were killed in my battle."

"That's pretty fair; but the war in Italy this summer will be no boys' play, and I want to be in it, either as an actor or a spectator."

"Very well; we are off to-night, then."

During the day we wrote our letters, drew what money we needed, and, as we were going to a troubled region, we sewed napoleons into our suspenders, waistbands, and other available places, so that we need not be deprived of the "sinews of war," in case of accident. At the time indicated, we were at the railroad station, where we found Cuore, as bland and polite, and as ready to serve us, as ever. Though the train was rather crowded, we obtained a compartment to ourselves by his skill and address, and we began to realize the benefit of having such an "old stager" with us.

At noon the next day we were in Marseilles, where we embarked the same evening for Nice.

CHAPTER XII.

IN WHICH PHIL AND LARRY CONTINUE THEIR JOURNEY, AND MEET A FRENCH GENERAL OF BRIGADE.

WE were in Marseilles about six hours, and had time to obtain a general view of the city. Cuore followed us wherever we went, and seemed to know the place as well as if he had lived there all his life. The steamer in which we embarked was French, and though she was crowded with passengers on their way to the seat of war, our zealous friend obtained the best accommodations on board for us. Larry and myself were exceedingly grateful to him for his attention. The sea was delightfully smooth, and the course of the vessel was in sight of the land. We remained on deck till it was too dark to see anything, and then retired to the cabin.

"You will drink a bottle of champagne with me now — won't you, gentlemen?" said Cuore, as we entered the cabin.

"I thank you, sir; but I never drink champagne, or any other wine," I replied.

"Nor I, either," added Larry, shrugging his shoulders, as though he regarded his refusal as an excellent joke.

"Americans are very singular people," laughed the Italian. "You must drink wine in Italy. The water will make you sick; and besides, it is warm and not pleasant to drink."

"I think I can stand it. I was brought up on river water. At any rate, I shall be sick a while before I drink any wine," I continued.

"But everybody drinks wine in Italy," persisted Cuore.

"No; I don't."

"Nor I," laughed my friend.

Larry and I went to our state-room, and very likely the Italian drank his champagne before he retired.

"Why should that fellow take so much pains to please us?" asked Larry, as we were turning in.

"I don't know, unless it is out of the kindness of his own heart," I replied.

"That's all in your eye, Phil. I never drank much champagne, but I have been about enough

to notice that when some fellows have a big
axe to grind, they use champagne for the grindstone."

"Possibly it may be so in this instance; at any rate, we will keep our eyes wide open. There is one thing about it, Larry: we are not likely to be blinded with champagne."

My friend's suggestion seemed to be worthy of consideration, and while I was thinking about it I dropped asleep, and did not wake till the wheels of the steamer stopped in the port of Nice. We went on shore, and taking a carriage, drove to the *Hôtel de la Méditerranée*, which is a very pleasant situation, facing the sea. I had chosen this hotel, and insisted upon going there, because my cousin's letter had informed me that my mother had boarded there, though Cuore desired to stay at the *Hôtel des Etrangers*. Even the fact of being at the place where my mother had spent the winter made me feel nearer to her than I had ever consciously been before. I had with me the precious memorials by which my father had been enabled to identify me, and I hoped soon to place them before my other parent.

Mr. Collingsby, my grandfather, and Mr. Collingsby, my uncle, had persistently refused even to consider my relationship to them, or to glance at the testimony I was able to produce. My mother had been in Europe nearly three years, with her brother, Joseph Collingsby, and his wife. I had never seen this uncle, but I supposed he must be as prudent, dignified, and unsentimental as the rest of the family whom I had met. It was even possible that he would not permit me to state my case to my mother; but I was determined not to fail in my undertaking. My first and only business in Nice was to obtain tidings of my mother, and as soon as I reached the hotel, I went to work upon the case. I applied at once to that important personage about European hotels, the porter, who had an office at the entrance. He spoke English, as well as three or four other languages.

"Did Mr. Joseph Collingsby board at this hotel during the winter?" I inquired.

"Yes, sir; an American, you mean?" replied the porter.

"Yes; who were with him?"

"Mrs. Collingsby and another lady — what was her name?"

The man opened his register, and began to turn the leaves.

"The party left about four weeks ago to go to Milan with Signor Bertani and family. Here is the lady's name — Mrs. Farringford."

The sight of the name sent my heart into my throat, and it did not at that moment occur to me that hostile armies lay between Nice and Milan.

"Is the lady in Milan now?" I inquired.

"I don't know, but I think so. Signor Bertani's family spent the winter here, and they were very intimate with the Collingsby party. Signor Bertani is a very rich Italian gentleman, and has a fine house in Milan. The Collingsbys were to stay a month or two with them, and then all of them were going to Switzerland; for the two gentlemen talked about the matter in my hearing. You wish to see Mr. Collingsby?"

"Mrs. Farringford, more particularly."

"You can't go to Milan now," added the porter.

"Perhaps I can."

"Signor Bertani made his fortune out of the Austrians, and he is not in favor of United Italy," continued the man, whose manner allowed no doubt in regard to his politics.

"I am sorry he is on the wrong side," I replied. "But can you tell me where to find him, in case I get to Milan?"

"He is a banker, Corso di Bosinare, No. 21," replied the porter, writing out the address in full. "The less you say about Signor Bertani, the better it will be for you, unless you are among the Austrians."

I paid but little attention to this friendly warning, and afterwards wished I had heeded it. To me the political question was a very plain one, and all my sympathies were with France and Italy. I believed in Cavour, the great Italian statesman, and his policy. Lombardy was clearly a part of Italy, and it seemed to me that Austria had no right there. The people wished to be restored to their natural political connections, and on the part of the Italians it was "freedom's battle" which was then in progress.

My business in Nice was accomplished; but we were obliged to remain in the city till the next forenoon, when a steamer left for Genoa.

"I consider myself very fortunate, Larry," said I, as we seated ourselves on deck to watch the shores of Italy, after the steamer had started.

"You always are, Phil; but I don't see wherein you are particularly so just now," replied he.

"I have ascertained just where my mother has gone."

"Not much luck in that; but I haven't much of an idea that you will get to Milan this summer, unless you join the French army, and go in with the soldiers."

"I would even do that for the sake of getting there."

"But when the allied army goes in, your mother will not be there, if she goes with the Austrians."

"I don't believe my mother goes with the Austrians; but I intend to find her, wherever she goes."

"You are a brick, Phil. Suppose we join the French army. That will be the easiest way to get into Milan this summer. I really want to take a part in this business," said Larry.

"Of course I couldn't think of such a thing. It would spoil all my plans."

"I want to get into something exciting."

"Perhaps we shall have that without going into the army. By the way, have you an idea that Cuore had any business in Nice?"

"If he had, he must have neglected it, for I don't think he was out of my sight five minutes at any one time."

"I was thinking of that this morning. He sticks to us like a leech."

"That's so; but he said he was going to Nice before you said anything about it. He did not come here for our sakes."

"He seems to keep good company," I added, pointing to a part of the deck where a group of officers stood, the principal one of whom was talking with Cuore.

"He is not a bashful man, like myself," laughed Larry. "He seems to be on good terms with that general of brigade."

"Is that his rank?"

"So Cuore told me."

The general was certainly a good-looking man, and apparently a very affable one. I was surprised to see our Italian friend so intimate with him; but if he was in the employ of the government, perhaps it was not very strange that he should be on speaking terms with a general of brigade in time of war. Larry and I turned in at an early hour, and I was soon asleep. I waked once in the night, and found that the little steamer was pitching violently in a head sea. The weather had been rather threatening when we retired, and I expected both wind and rain during the night. But I was accustomed to a stormy sea, and turning over in my berth, I went to sleep again. Early in the morning Larry waked me.

"It blows great guns, Phil," said he.

"Let it blow," I replied, still quite sleepy.

"I don't know that we can help ourselves," he added; "but I have been up half the night."

"What for?"

"I couldn't sleep. The steamer rolled so, my brains were nearly knocked out. The French brigadier was on deck; and if ever a brave man was frightened, he was."

"There is no occasion to be alarmed."

"I am not alarmed; for I told you I was as ready to live as die. I was speaking of the brigadier. He was on the hurricane deck, holding on to the bob-stay."

"Was he, indeed? Then he has tremendous long arms," I added, laughing at Larry's blunder.

"Well, the brig-stay, then."

"I never heard of that stay before. Probably

it was the mizzen-stay; for there is such a piece of rigging within reach of the hurricane deck."

"The brigadier had to stay there, whatever the stay was. The steamer dipped the water in over her sides as she rolled, and *monsieur* expected to go to the bottom. I had quite a chat with him, for he speaks English first rate. He's going directly to the front."

"I'm willing; but if you have been up half the night, Larry, you had better turn in again, and finish your nap. Your berth is the most comfortable place when it blows."

"I don't think so; I want to see the fun, and cultivate the acquaintance of the brigadier. I thought you might want to know what's going on; so I waked you. Who knows but I may get a chance on the brigadier's staff. I know all about soldiering, for I was a high private in the Forty-ninth for nearly a year. If I could only speak the lingo, I would go in."

I don't know what else my friend said, for I dropped asleep again. I was not much interested in his military aspirations, and I concluded that his want of fluency in the language would be a sufficient bar to all his hopes. But Larry had improved his French wonderfully, for he had bought a phrase book in Paris, which he studied during a large portion of the time, practising with Cuore and myself. I slept till the steamer's wheels stopped, and then went on deck. The boat was two hours late, and when I joined Larry she was inside of the two long moles which protect the harbor of Genoa. The port was crowded with French and Italian transport steamers, which had brought in troops and stores from Marseilles, Toulon, and Leghorn, and our vessel was obliged to anchor near the jaws of the harbor. The wind was south-east, and still blowing a gale, which made a heavy sea, even inside of the moles. But rough as the sea was, the shore boats came off for passengers; for I believe there is not a single Mediterranean port where vessels go up to a quay or wharf.

Larry was talking with the general, who still held on at the mizzen-stay, and his military coat was soaked by the spray and rain.

"Here is Phil," said he, as soon as I appeared on deck. "He knows all about it."

I walked up to him.

"General Eberlé, this is my friend, Mr. Farringford," continued Larry.

The general gave me his hand, and greeted me warmly, though he did not release his hold of the stay with his left hand, and I noticed that he kept one eye on the surging waves.

"Can we go to ze shore in ze little boat?" he asked, anxiously, as he glanced at the small craft, whose owners were vociferously offering their services. "*Votre ami a dit que vous îtes marin.*"

"*Oui, monsieur;* you can land very well," I replied.

"I have very much fear of ze watair."

"There is not much danger, sir, if the boats are well managed."

I said what I could to assure the general that a boat could live in the sea around us, but I was willing to admit that it was not without peril. I presumed that the boatmen were skilful in their business. He was very anxious to leave the steamer, and we engaged two boats to land us. They were small craft, and were manned by father and son, the latter of whom was a boy of sixteen. General Eberlé and another officer went with the old man, while Larry and I, with our baggage, took passage with the boy. Cuore and an officer engaged a third boat. We embarked safely, and in another moment we were bobbing up and down like feathers on the angry waves. A combing wave broke over the stern of the old man's boat, which startled the general, and he did the stupidest thing a man could possibly do under such circumstances, for he sprang to his feet. I heard the boatman shout, and then I saw the brigadier topple over into the water. He disappeared from my sight for a moment, and then I discovered him struggling on the top of a huge wave.

"Give way, man!" I shouted to our boatman; but he appeared to be paralyzed by the catastrophe, and did not understand English.

Finding he could do nothing, I sprang from the bow of the boat where I was seated, and grasped the oars. Driving the boy forward, I pulled the boat up to the unfortunate general. But just at that moment his head bobbed under. I brought the little craft up head to the sea, and then told the boy, in French, to take the oars again. Perhaps he understood my gestures better than my words; at any rate, he obeyed me, and I returned to the bow.

"Keep still, Larry! Don't move!" I shouted to my friend, whose movements indicated that he intended to jump overboard. "I will get him in a minute."

The general rose again, and I fastened the boat-hook into his military coat, and hauled him up to the bow. By this time the old man had come to the rescue, and with his aid the unfortunate man was hauled into his boat, which was nearly swamped in the act.

CHAPTER XIII.

IN WHICH PHIL AND LARRY BECOME SOLDIERS, AND SPEND THEIR FIRST NIGHT IN BIVOUAC.

IT seems almost incredible that a man so brave as General Eberlé proved himself to be in the fiery onslaught of battle should be timid under any circumstances. I have heard of a sea captain who never knew what fear was in a gale, on the deck of his own ship, but who was absolutely terrified in a small sail-boat, when the wind was simply fresh. The general was certainly frightened, and had practically thrown himself overboard; but the old Italian had him safe in the bottom of his boat now; and I saw him gesticulating violently to his distinguished passenger, in order to keep him quiet in his place.

Neither the old man nor the young man was willing to come about in that heavy sea; for we were now in the most exposed position. Taking a sharp angle with the direction of the waves, they brought their boats under the lee of the steamer, and there came about. Keeping well in towards the shore, where the water was partially sheltered by the mole, they landed at the custom-house quay. General Eberlé went on shore first, and as soon as Larry and I joined him, he rushed towards me, threw himself upon me, and hugged me as though I had been his lost baby. I was not a little startled at the demonstrative Frenchman's method of testifying his gratitude.

"You have saved my life!" exclaimed he, first in French and then in English.

"That's so," said Larry.

"You know ze boat; you know ze sea, Monsieur Farringford. You have saved my life!" repeated the general, hugging me again.

I submitted, with the best grace I could, to this loving treatment; but I protested that I had done nothing to deserve such an expression of emotion.

"You have saved my life. You have saved to France and Italy a general of brigade. I shall fight well with ze life you have given to me."

"I have no doubt you will."

"I have no fear on ze battle-ground; but I have

very much fear in ze boat," added the general, apologetically. "Now we will go to ze Hotel Feder, if you please."

"I have some baggage."

But my trunk passed the officers without opening, and in a few moments we reached the hotel. The general told me he had just come from Algiers, and had been assigned to a command in the army in Italy.

"I wish to go to Milan," said I, after my new friend had restated his obligations to me.

"It is not possible now; but the army will be in Milan in one or two weeks. You shall go with the army. I will take care of you myself."

"Thank you; and I will accept your offer," I replied, promptly.

He left me to change his wet clothes for dry ones. He had hardly left the room before Cuore came to me, though he had not been out of my sight since we landed at the custom-house.

"Now we shall go to Milan," said the Italian, rubbing his hands, as if delighted with the prospect.

"General Eberlé says it is quite impossible," I answered.

"To him, yes; to me, no," added the Italian.

"I have accepted his kind invitation to go there with the army, which will be in Milan within a week or two."

"You have accepted his invitation!" exclaimed Cuore, with a sudden start of astonishment.

"I have."

"What for have you done this?" he demanded, with an ugly look, such as I had not before seen on his face.

I thought he manifested more feeling about the matter than the occasion required; and I could not but ask myself again why he had taken so much pains to please us.

"Because I think the army will take me to Milan," I replied.

"But the army may never get to Milan," protested Cuore, who had never hinted at such a possibility before, and who had all along professed to believe that the allies would march straight across the plains of Lombardy, as soon as they were ready.

"Don't you expect the Austrians will be beaten in this campaign?" I asked, quietly.

"Nothing is sure, you know. The Austrians have many soldiers and good generals."

"You seem to have changed your tone, Signor Cuore."

"No; but it will be a long time before the army enters Milan."

"Well, I have agreed to go with the general."

"And your friend?"

"Of course we shall keep together."

"But I have engaged to take you to Milan."

"Have you? We will release you from the obligation, then. But I am not aware of the existence of any agreement on the subject. As you were going to Nice, and then to Milan, and we were going to the same places, we have come together."

"But I have pledged myself to take you to Milan," replied he, warmly.

"I did not know it before."

"And if you go with me, you shall be in Milan in three days, at the most," said he, in a kind of imploring tone, as though it was a matter of some consequence that we should go with him.

"The allied army and the Austrian army lie between us and Milan. Will you tell me how you intend to pass both lines?" I inquired.

"Hist! Not so loud. You must not speak of these things."

"We are alone."

"The Austrians have spies everywhere," whispered Cuore.

It was afterwards shown that the Austrians were sadly deficient in this important branch of the military service.

"I shall not start on an expedition through the lines of either army without knowing anything about the means of passing through."

"I shall be your guide and friend."

"I have no desire to be shot with you as a spy, if you are."

"We shall not be shot if you trust to me. I know every rod of ground from Genoa to Milan; and I have the passes," added Cuore, in a whisper.

"Come, Phil, we are off in an hour," said Larry, joining me in the dining-room, where I was waiting for breakfast. "Hurry up the grub; the general is about ready."

"I have helped you through so far; I have got the best cabins in the steamers for you; I have done all I could for you."

"You have been very kind, and we are greatly obliged to you for your favors."

"Precisely so," added Larry.

"And now you will leave me?"

"That depends upon which way you are going. If you are going with us, we don't leave you, any more than a man parts with his head. That's so, 'pon my soul!" said my friend, lightly.

The entrance of the general terminated the conversation, and we sat down to breakfast. I pointed to a chair for Cuore; but to my surprise, he begged to be excused, and took his meal alone, in another part of the room. In explanation of his conduct, I learned, afterwards, that he did not consider it proper for him to sit at table with a general of brigade. After breakfast we departed in a military train, and in a few hours arrived at Alessandria, which was a strongly fortified city, the citadel being quite a town of itself. The place was crowded with French soldiers, for it was the left of the line on the Po, by which the emperor intended at first to invade Lombardy. He had now just changed his plan, though I knew nothing of it at the time, and was moving his army up towards the line of the Ticino. Troops were constantly arriving and departing; but the general soon ascertained that his brigade was in the vicinity of Vercelli.

"The whole plan is changed," said Cuore, in a solemn and mysterious manner. "I shall go to the Lago Maggiore, and into Milan from the north. I intended to go by Pavia."

"What do you mean by the plan being changed?" I asked.

"Don't you see that all the troops are moving towards the north?"

"I haven't the least idea which way they are moving."

"Pardon; the train is ready," said General Eberlé, politely interruping the conversation.

We took our places with the general in the troop train; but Cuore did not enter the compartment with us, though we knew he was not far away.

"General, do you know Signor Cuore?" I asked, as the train moved off.

"No," replied he, shrugging his shoulders in the true French style.

"I saw you talking with him on board of the steamer."

"I have never seen ze man till then. No; he is in ze government service, he say," added the general, laughing, and with his significant shrug im-

The Bivouac of the French Army. Page 185.

plied that more was to be understood than was expressed. "He only tell me ze news."

In two hours more the train stopped in the fields. The ground, as far as we could see, was covered with the camps of the French and Sardinian troops. Our military friend told us we were near the front. We walked about a mile, to the headquarters of the general of division, where the brigadier reported himself. An aid then conducted us to a farm-house, at least two miles distant, and the general took possession of his headquarters, relieving the officer in command. I watched all the formalities with interest, after the brigade was drawn up. Cuore was close at my side, but Larry remained in the farm-house for a short time. When I was beginning to wonder what had become of him, General Eberlé and his staff rode by me. Of the latter there were only three or four; but, to my utter astonishment, not to say dismay, I recognized Larry as one of them! He wore an undress uniform, was well mounted, and looked as much like a Frenchman as any of them. As he passed me he smiled, and gave me the military salute. I concluded that this was the result of the long conversations with the general.

"He will not go to Milan!" exclaimed Cuore, who still clung to me like a brother.

"Probably he intends to go with the army," I replied.

"This is very bad; he will not go to Milan with us," muttered the Italian, evidently more disgusted at Larry's conduct than I was.

"You and I can go alone, then," I suggested.

"You will not leave your friend."

"No; but he appears to be leaving me."

I felt like a cat in a strange garret after the discovery I had made. The Italian for a time was my only companion, and he was even more discontented than I was. When the parade was dismissed, I went back to the farm-house, which had a picture of the Virgin and three saints painted over the front door. The stable was connected with the house, and was filled with officers' horses. It was two hours before the general and Larry came in to dinner.

I must say that my friend made a fine-looking officer, and did not stumble over the sword that dangled at his side.

"What in the world have you been doing, Larry?" I exclaimed, as soon as I had a chance to speak to him.

"I've been going in for United Italy," laughed he. "It was quite impossible for me to keep my fingers out of this pie."

"But what is your position?" I asked, curiously.

"Volunteer aid-de-camp, without pay. Didn't you hear the adjutant read my appointment on parade?"

"No, I didn't notice it. You are a pretty aid-de-camp! How can you deliver the general's orders, when you don't understand the language, and no Frenchman could comprehend you, if you did?"

"The general speaks English, and he will write his orders," laughed Larry. "Come, Phil, there's another place, just like mine, for you."

"For me! I don't know the first thing about military."

"Not necessary to know anything. You can't go to Milan with the army in a civilian's dress."

"I will think of it," I replied, tempted by this consideration.

I could not understand how it was possible to appoint an utterly incompetent person even as a volunteer aid-de-camp; but the general alone was responsible for this; and I realized that he only desired to do me a favor, and evidently expected nothing of me. To my surprise, after the disgust he had manifested at Larry's conduct, Cuore advised, and even pleaded, that I should accept the offer.

"You will have nothing to do, either of you, except to look on. The general gives you the position for your own protection and comfort, because you saved his life in the Bay of Genoa," said he. "You can go and come as you please; and very likely your position will enable you to get into Milan sooner than without it."

Though I was rather inclined to distrust my Italian friend, I thought he was right, and I accepted the offer. I promptly purchased a uniform, as Larry had done, of a sutler. It was a second-hand affair, and a hole in the breast of the coat suggested the fate of its former owner; but it had been thoroughly renovated, and I was entirely satisfied with it. The sutler declared that the hole in the breast of the coat made it worth ten francs more, for the owner could point to it as an evidence of his courage; but, of course, any one could shoot a hole through his coat, and thus make himself a hero.

I had left my trunk in Genoa, transferring a few

articles, including the relics of my childhood, with which I never parted, to a small bag. I made a bundle of my travelling suit, and strapped it to the bag, for I did not think I should long remain a soldier. I was not a little astonished when I found myself transformed into a military man; and I surveyed myself all over to observe the effect. I was decidedly in favor of the cause which I had thus lightly espoused, and if its success had depended upon my arm, or even my life, I would not have been backward.

My position did not seem real to me, and I felt like a spectator rather than an actor in the exciting events which were transpiring around me. I did not feel called upon to expose myself to the perils of battle, and I was too ignorant of the military art to be of any service in the brigade. We remained at this camp two days, during which Larry was busy every moment of the time, hardly allowing himself the needed hours of rest. On the day after our arrival he came to me with a couple of muskets in his hands, and insisted upon my taking one of them. He then put me through a portion of the manual, using the French words of command. When I expressed my surprise, he told me that he had been taking lessons of an orderly sergeant, on duty at headquarters. I soon learned to handle a musket, and, by observing the drills and parades, obtained a knowledge of the French technical terms. Of course my stock of military science was very slight indeed, though I could not help adding to it almost every moment.

On the third day after our arrival all the troops appeared to be in motion, and our brigade was soon on the march. Larry had purchased a horse for his own use, though I declined to waste my money in following his example; but a steed was furnished for me. We moved forward in a north-easterly direction, over fields and vineyards, till nine o'clock in the evening, and then halted on the banks of a river. Tents and baggage had been left behind, and we spent the night in bivouac on the border of the stream.

CHAPTER XIV.

IN WHICH PHIL AND LARRY MOVE FORWARD WITH THE ARMY, AND DECIDE TO VISIT MILAN.

BY the kindness of General Eberlé, Larry and I were plentifully supplied with blankets, and I slept very well. It was not the first time I had passed the night in the open air, for I had often camped under a tree in the wilds of the Upper Missouri, with my old hunter friend. The army had been moving for two days, but I could not form the least idea of what was going on. Though everything was in perfect order, and every division and brigade was doing precisely what it had been directed to do, the whole movement appeared to me to be a mass of confusion. For two days more we moved about from place to place, apparently without object or aim, until we again bivouacked on the bank of the stream, which was the River Sesia. I heard that the King of Sardinia was on one side of us, and the Emperor of France on the other; but I did not see either of them that day.

On the following morning, for the first time, I heard the rattle of musketry and the roar of cannon, on the other side of the river. This was the battle of Palestro. The King of Sardinia had crossed the river the day before, and the Austrians were now attacking him in the position he had taken. The fight was long and severe, but the Austrians were handsomely repulsed on the front, though they succeeded in flanking the Italians on the right, and the result for a time looked very doubtful. This part of the conflict we could see from our position, and our men were anxious to take part in it. Larry was intensely excited, and declared that the Austrians had won the day. The general thought not, for the French could throw in twenty thousand men, if needed, to turn the tide. We saw the Austrians post their batteries on a rising ground, which some accounts of the battle describe as a hill, though there is no such thing in this part of Lombardy. At the foot of the slope was a canal, which conveyed the waters of the Sesia to a mill. Across this canal rushed the Third French Zouaves, some of them on the narrow plank bridge, and others through the muddy waters. They were dashing fellows, and on they went up the slope, under a sharp fire of artillery and musketry. I saw many of the brave fellows drop on the way; but almost in the twinkling of an eye they had captured the Austrian position, taking the guns and many prisoners, and driving hundreds of the enemy into the canal.

The field was won, and a score of ringing cheers, short and sharp, rent the air. The Austrians who were in condition to do so fled. In the evening they rallied, and made an attempt to retake the place, but were completely repulsed.

"What do you think of that, Phil?" said Larry, after the Zouave charge.

"I think it was well done."

"So do I; but I don't like to stand here looking on," he added, impatiently.

"This is the safest position."

"Humph! That isn't what I bargained for. I want to hear the bullets whistle."

"I am perfectly satisfied to be at a safe distance. Bullets that whistle have an ugly habit of boring through one's bones and meat, and making the blood run."

"That is what makes it exciting business. If there were no danger, there would be no fun."

"I don't desire that sort of fun."

"I do."

"Do you suppose Blanche Fennimore has any particular regard for you, Larry?"

"I happen to know that she has," replied he, promptly.

"If she knew that you were trying to throw away your life in a struggle of this kind, do you think she would be comforted by the knowledge?"

"'None but the brave deserve the fair.' She will think ten times as much of me if I behave like a man."

"But you have no particular interest in this quarrel. You go into it as a mere adventurer, because you like excitement."

"I have a particular interest in it. I always go in for the bottom dog, and I am willing to go in for any people that are oppressed by their rulers. Where would our country — or your country, I suppose I must call it now — have been, if the French hadn't stepped in to help you out?"

"I don't know; but perhaps we should have come out all right."

"Perhaps you would — only you wouldn't."

"The French were fighting their own battle while they were fighting ours. They took our part because they hated England, rather than because they loved us, though this fact does not relieve us of the debt of gratitude we owe to France. If you behave as well as you talk, Larry, I am afraid you will be shot."

"I will bet you a supper for the crowd that I don't get shot."

"Bet! That would be trifling with the mercy of God."

"I dare say you are right, Phil. You ought to have been a parson."

"Don't bet on anything, Larry; least of all, on a matter so serious as the chances of life; for we are always in the hands of our Father."

"But the chances of being shot are really less than you think, Phil."

"There are chances enough, at least."

After supper, we crossed the river, and bivouacked on the other side. The next morning we marched to Novara, and encamped outside of the walls. It was evident to all that we were on the eve of a great battle, for Milan was less than thirty miles distant, and the Austrians would not allow the capital of Lombardy to be occupied by the allies without a desperate attempt to save it. Our general thought we were near the centre of the line, and that in less than three days we should see some very heavy fighting. I was not particularly pleased with the prospect, especially as I found that my military friend was somewhat inclined to use me. On parade, and elsewhere, I carried orders, and it seemed to me that I was an errand-boy on a large scale. I did not object to being an aid-de-camp in the reserve, if this portion of the force was not called into action.

"There will be lively times here soon, Phil," said Larry, as we met at sunset.

"I'm not anxious to see any such times as you suggest," I replied. "In fact, I'm rather sorry that I put on this uniform."

"Come, Phil, don't back down."

"I haven't backed down; but I don't want to be shot, or to be thrown into an Austrian prison."

"Are you afraid?"

"I am — a downright coward in this business; for I feel that it does not particularly concern me."

"You are honest, Phil; but I don't believe you are a coward."

"I am."

"Impossible!" said a voice behind us, which we identified as that of Cuore.

We had not seen him before for three days, and I supposed he was on his mission within the Austrian lines.

"I thought you were on the other side of the Ticino," I suggested.

"I have been; but I have come back. I have been in Milan," replied the Italian.

"Indeed!"

"I left Milan last night."

"Last night!" I exclaimed, astonished at the facility with which he seemed to pass through the hostile lines. "How could you have come through so soon?"

"The trains on the railroad run down as far as Magenta, to bring supplies for the troops; from there I came in a baggage wagon nearly to the Ticino River. I am going back again to-night."

"To Milan?"

"Yes."

Cuore was very fluent in his speech, and did not seem to be at all fatigued by his long journey and the excitement of passing through the pickets of both armies. He seemed to me to be a wonderful fellow, and I could form some idea of the importance of the man to the French arms, for doubtless he had informed the generals of the precise location and numbers of the Austrians. I was strongly impressed by his skill and powers of endurance, and I gazed at him with wonder and astonishment.

"I passed through the Corso di Bosinare, while I was in Milan," he added, as I was still regarding him.

"What's that?" I asked.

"Don't you remember?"

"No."

"Signor Bertani," he continued, suggestively.

"Ah, did you, indeed? It was very kind of you to think of me, when you had so much business on your hands," I replied, recalling the name as the friend of my mother, and of the Collingsbys, to whom he alluded.

"I never forget or neglect a friend."

"Did you obtain any information?" I asked, deeply interested in the matter.

"I did; I spoke with Signor Bertani himself."

"Are his American friends still with him?"

"They are, and are likely to remain with him; for, you see, it is quite impossible to get into Switzerland, by any direct route, for Garibaldi and the *Chasseurs d'Alpes* hold the lakes, and have possession of all the steamers. Besides, the Austrians in Milan do not expect to lose the city."

"But suppose the city should be captured; would Signor Bertani leave?" I inquired.

"Certainly he would; the Italians would hang him if they caught him."

"Would his family depart?"

"I think not. If Milan is captured, the Austrians will want all the railway carriages for their own use, and would not give them up for women and children, who would be perfectly safe in the city. But you should go to Milan before the army."

"Why so?"

"You will be sure to find your mother now; but if you wait two or three days the Austrians may fortify the city. Then the French will bombard it, and the women and children must all leave."

"Do you think I could pass through the lines?" I asked, somewhat excited by such a prospect.

"You can pass safely through with me. I will promise that both of you shall be in Milan before six o'clock to-morrow morning."

"I cannot go," interposed Larry.

"Not go with your friend?" said Cuore.

"No; I am going to see that big battle, and have a finger in the pie, too. I shall not leave the army," added Larry, very decidedly.

"I thought you would keep together," continued the Italian, who seemed to be strangely vexed and disturbed at the decision of my friend.

"Never mind me, Phil. Go ahead with him, and I shall see you when we get to Milan," said Larry.

"But I can take the two better than one," answered Cuore.

"How's that?" I inquired.

"I have a pass for three persons," said he, taking a paper from his pocket, which he showed to me.

It was written in German, and he knew that I was entirely ignorant of that language. He permitted me to see it, but not to take it from his hands.

"Let me see it," added Larry. "I will take it to our orderly. He is a Swiss, and speaks German like a Dutchman. Let me take it."

"No — pardon; I must not let my pass go out of my own hands," replied Cuore, folding up the paper and returning it to his pocket. "I must be very prudent. I am in the employ of the Austrians as well as the French; but I give them only such information as will be useful to United Italy."

Cuore chuckled, and looked very cunning. It seemed very strange to me that a pass which would answer for three persons would not do for two; and I expressed myself to this effect.

"Ah, you see I have promised to bring over to the Austrian general two men who can tell better than I where the French are posted. You can tell him; but, of course, you will not give him any correct information. I have obtained this pass for you, and both must go, or neither."

"I can't go, Phil," said Larry.

"You may return before the great battle takes place," suggested Cuore. "There may be no fight for a week."

"And there may be one to-morrow."

"No, not possible. The allies are not in position to fight a battle yet."

"No one can know when it will come off. I dare say his majesty the Emperor of France has laid his plans well, for he is a very clever fellow; but even he cannot tell when the battle will be fought. He may intend to set the ball rolling in three days, or a week; but, I take it, the Austrians may have a finger in the pie, as well as the emperor and myself, and if they take a notion to fight a battle to-night even, we can't help ourselves. The emperor and I are not going to keep still, and let them whip us; so you see I can't go. It is morally, socially, and politically impossible," continued Larry.

"I can go without you," I replied.

"Certainly you can, Phil."

"If I have one, I must have two," persisted Cuore.

"Can't you tell the Austrian general that one of your men had a corn on his little toe, and couldn't come?"

"No," replied the Italian, shaking his head violently; and it was plain that he did not intend to visit Milan without my friend.

"Here's the general," said Larry. "We'll lay the matter before him."

My friend stated the case to General Eberlé, who at once declared that no battle was possible within twenty-four hours, and that the emperor would choose his own time, in spite of the Austrians.

"But this is very perilous business," he added.

"Then I would like to engage in it," said my obstinate friend.

"I can make it very safe," interposed Cuore, with the utmost deference.

The general turned to the Italian, and began to question him rather sharply in regard to his business in the camp. Cuore replied very promptly, and substantially in accordance with what he had said to us.

"Show the Austrian pass, signore," added Larry.

"No," interposed the general, walking away. "If he were not your friend, gentlemen, I would order ze arrest of ze man."

"But he is in the employ of the French," I replied.

"I don't know," answered the general, shrugging his shoulders.

"He brought information to General Canrobert, this morning, from Milan."

"I don't know; I can't say," added the general.

He declared that a spy could be known only to his immediate employers. He knew nothing about the man. If he saw an Austrian pass, he should be obliged to arrest him; therefore he would not see it. He seemed to have no opinion whatever in regard to Cuore, and left us free to do as we deemed advisable. I had some suspicions in regard to the Italian; but I could not trace them to any reasonable foundation. I discussed the matter for half an hour with Larry, and then we decided to visit Milan.

CHAPTER XV.

IN WHICH PHIL AND LARRY FLOAT DOWN THE CANAL,
AND ARE DISTURBED BY FRENCH PICKET GUARDS.

I HAD a certain confidence in Cuore, which led me to believe that he was able to do what he promised, though I was not willing to give myself blindly into his charge. The general knew nothing about him, and said nothing to weaken my confidence. I could not see why he should be so anxious to have Larry go to Milan, when my friend had no business there, as I had. We walked back to the place where we had left the Italian, and told him we were ready to depart. Of course anything like baggage was out of the question; but I had put the locket and bracelets of my childhood into a pocket inside of my vest, for I had not dared to leave these valuables in my bag at the camp. The shawl and the dress were in my trunk at Genoa.

"We are rather too early yet," said Cuore, as he glanced around him.

"Why too early?" I inquired.

"The less time we have to spare, the fewer questions we shall have to answer. I have a couple of letters I wish to post," added the Italian, thrusting his hands into his pockets. "I must send them to Novara."

"You can leave them at the camp. An orderly goes up to the town with the mail every day," said Larry. "Give them to me, and I will see that they are sent."

"I will go to the headquarters," replied Cuore, still fumbling in his pockets for the letters. "I must give the orderly the money to pay the postage."

We went to the house in which the brigade headquarters were located. Cuore gave his letters to the orderly, who put them in a leather bag which hung on the wall.

"Now we are ready to go," said Cuore. "We have a long walk before us, and I hope you are fresh and strong."

"I can walk all night," I replied.

"So can I; but hurry up your cakes, signore," added Larry.

"My cakes?" repeated the Italian. "I have been to supper."

"So have I; and therefore let us keep moving. We go as though we were attending the funeral of a general of division."

"We must not hurry. We shall pass the French lines about five kilomètres from here, and I do not wish to go through till about dark."

"Why not? If you have a pass for the crowd, what difference does it make?" replied Larry, impatiently.

"It will make much delay. I have a pass signed by General Canrobert; but—"

"Let me see it," interposed Larry.

"Not here; by and by, when we halt for a time, you shall see it. But I wish to go through the French line without showing the pass."

"Why so? Do you want to be shot?"

"No, no; of course I don't want to be shot. When it is dark I can get through with less delay. If I show the pass, the soldiers will send for the sergeant, the sergeant for the sous-lieutenant, he for the captain, the captain for the general of brigade, and the general of brigade for the general of division; then it must go to the field marshal, and from him to the emperor; and we shall not get through till to-morrow night."

"Then you are going to run through."

"Precisely so; but if any one stops us, I have the pass for three persons."

"If any one can go through the pickets as easily as you suggest, they don't amount to much," said Larry.

"You don't understand me."

"That's so; I don't."

"I know the country, and I have a grand plan to do this business right. You have seen some canals in this part of Italy."

"Plenty of them," answered Larry.

"You've seen that they have trees on each side."

"Yes; I haven't been over a ditch that did not have a row of trees or bushes on both sides."

"I shall bring you to a canal that runs into the river," continued Cuore.

"What river?" I asked.

"The Ticino, which flows into the Po near Pavia. This river is the picket line for the Austrians on one side, and the allies on the other; but neither line goes very near the river. On the canal, one kilomètre from the stream, I have a boat, in which I came over this morning — a petit bateau, in which we can float down to the river, in the shade of the trees, without being seen."

"Of course the pickets will hear the sound of the oars or paddle," suggested Larry.

"We shall use no oars."

"But the water in the canal must run from the river."

"No, no; it runs the other way."

"That's a humbug," protested Larry.

"What do you call humbug?"

"What's the canal for, if it don't run from the river?"

"It is to wet the land, to — what you call it? — to irritate — no; to — "

"Irrigate," I suggested.

"Ah, to irrigate the land! You are right. The canal flows from the river in one place, farther up, and comes back into the river in another place, below the first. From the big canal flow a great many small ones through the land, so that the water can be spread all over the fields."

"Precisely so; I understand it, Larry."

"So do I; and we will grant that the water in this part of the canal runs into the river."

"I have told you all the way then," resumed Cuore. "The flow of the water will take the little boat into the river. We cross over, and go into a canal on the other side."

"And I suppose that canal, to suit our convenience, runs from the river," laughed my friend.

"You are right," replied Cuore. "Its waters will carry us to a safe place. Then we walk up to Magenta, where there is very often a train for Milan."

"No doubt of it; everything seems to have been arranged especially for our convenience."

"Ah, you see, I know the country! That is the reason the French generals sent me on a mission for them," added the Italian, with much self-complacency.

"Do you expect to float down this canal without being noticed by the sentinels?" I inquired.

"I do; but what matter if we are noticed? You wear the uniform of French officers. If we are stopped I have only to show the pass of General Canrobert."

I had become so accustomed to the military salute, greeting us at almost every step of our walk, which, of course, Larry and I returned, that I had almost forgotten my existence as a civilian. We passed from one camp to another without difficulty, for our uniform was all the pass we required. It did not occur to me then that we were conducting Cuore, instead of the reverse, until, when we had finished our conversation, and the Italian walked a little ahead of us, he was challenged by the sentinel. A word from Larry, bad French as it was, enabled him to pass.

We walked our five kilomètres, or about three miles, and reached the canal which our guide had described. It was half a mile from the nearest camp, where the last line of sentinels was posted, and the space between it and the river was patroled by pickets. On the other side of the stream, Austrian guns were posted behind fieldworks. The country was covered with long lines of mulberry trees, between which, in the same row, were grape-vines trained up between the trees. The land had been sown with grain, but the march of armies had been over it, so that the crop was ruined.

Cuore led us to a point on the canal which was overgrown with osiers, from which the owner evidently obtained his basket-stock. Just above it a party of French officers were bathing. Among the osiers lay the boat. It was a flat-bottom affair, half full of water. We dragged it up and turned it over, but it did not look like a very promising craft for a long cruise.

"It leaks badly," said Larry.

"No; not at all," replied Cuore. "I filled it with water to prevent the soldiers from taking it."

"I say, signore, if you mean to drown us, say so in the beginning," added Larry, glancing at the frail bateau.

"No, you cannot be drowned. The water is not deep in the canal, and not deep in the river. I have come two miles in that boat this morning."

"The boat is well enough," I interposed, as I seated myself in the forward part.

"Whatever you say about boats, Phil, I believe," added my friend, taking his place in the stern.

"Now you will take these," continued Cuore, drawing a couple of fish-poles from the osiers.

"O, then this is a fishing excursion—is it?" exclaimed Larry, as he examined the hook and line.

"Yes; the pickets will make no trouble when they see two officers fishing in the canal, or in the river."

"I say, signore, is there any danger of catching a fish here?"

"Plenty of fish here."

"I like fishing; but we have no bait."

"Yes, there is bait in the tin box under the seat."

Larry opened the box, and found a variety of live bugs, one of which he impaled on his hook. I dropped my line to him, and he baited my hook in the same manner.

"Now let the boat float down the canal, and don't use the oars," said Cuore.

"But are you not going with us?" I asked, when I saw by his movements that we were to be alone.

"Not yet; I will get into the boat in a few moments. The current will hardly move you, and I wish to see where the picket line is. I will not lose sight of you. Don't be alarmed," said Cuore, in a low tone.

"Where are you going?" demanded Larry.

"Only a short distance from the canal. When I see just where the pickets are, I can manage it better. I wish them not to see us till we get into the river."

"Then they will fire upon us," I suggested.

"No, they will not. They will see that you are French officers."

"But the Austrians will."

"No, no, no; the Austrians expect us. They know we are coming," answered the Italian, impatiently, as he pushed off the boat, and disappeared behind the osiers.

We did not see him again very soon.

The boat floated out into the canal, which was not more than ten feet wide. We dropped our lines overboard. Our craft hardly moved.

"I have a bite!" exclaimed Larry.

"Pull him in, then!"

"Lost him! Well, that's just my luck. If I bait for anything I never catch it."

"But the fish jump into your basket, without giving you the trouble to catch them. In a few years, more or less, you will be Sir Lawrence Grimsby; and I suppose you won't know such small fish as I am then."

"Dry up, Phil! You are the first real friend I ever had. You lend me money and tell me I am a vagabond in the same instant. I don't talk gratitude, or any such bosh; but — no matter; I have another bite. Gone again, as usual!"

"I wonder where Cuore is," I added, not feeling much interest in fishing, while our boat was bearing us slowly towards the hostile lines.

"I don't know. You never bet, Phil, nor I, since I knew you. But six months ago, I would have gone three against two that this Cuore is a knave."

"Do you think so?"

"I do, 'pon my soul."

"I have had some suspicions."

"So have I; but I can't make it out; so I try to think he is all right," replied Larry. "What is the fellow driving at? Why is he so anxious that I should go to Milan, when I haven't the least desire to go there at present?"

"I don't understand him; and I don't see through this business. Why should he leave us floating down this canal alone?"

"I don't know. I don't like to back out of anything, Phil; but I expect, as soon as we get to the river, to have a bullet put through my cap. I don't think it will go through my head, because a man that is born to be hanged won't be shot."

"I am willing to back out any time when it is not safe to go ahead. I have no fancy whatever for having an Austrian bullet go through even my cap. In my case, however it may be with you, I am afraid it would go through my head also."

I dropped my fishing tackle, and picked up an oar, with which I pushed the boat up to the bank.

"O, let her slide a while longer! The French pickets will not fire at us. Just attend to your fishing; we are safe enough in the canal," said Larry, laughing at my fears.

"I believe in backing out in good season."

"There is time enough. Cuore may, after all, be an honest man, though I don't know of any particular reason why he should be so anxious to help us into Milan. Has he asked you for any money?"

"No; he never even hinted at payment for anything," I replied.

"If he means anything, of course it is to make some money out of us; but he wouldn't make anything by letting the Austrians shoot us, for I haven't a big pile with me."

I permitted the boat to float again with the current, but I was fully resolved not to venture

THE ARREST OF PHIL AND LARRY. Page 217.

upon the river, unless the Italian should give me some stronger assurance than we had yet received of his ability to protect us. We had not yet examined his pass from Canrobert, but it was still light enough to do so. We continued on our course till I saw the river ahead. We looked about for the Italian, but he was not to be seen.

"This is as far as I will go, Larry," I said, taking the oar again, when the boat was within fifty yards of the river.

"I'm with you, Phil."

"We will wait here till Cuore comes back," I replied, pushing the bateau to the bank.

"Perhaps the fellow has been arrested himself — who knows?" laughed Larry.

"It is not improbable. He walked through several lines of sentinels on the strength of our uniforms."

"If he has been arrested, of course we don't go to Milan to-night," said Larry.

"*Non, messieurs ; vous ne pouvez pas aller à Milan cette nuit,*" said a French soldier, rising from the ground, and pointing his musket at my head.

Three others appeared at the same moment, and

imitated the dangerous example of the speaker, who had said, "No, gentlemen, you cannot go to Milan to-night."

"Here we are, Phil," said Larry, shrugging his shoulders.

CHAPTER XVI.

IN WHICH PHIL AND LARRY DISCUSS THE SITUATION,
AND FACE A DRUM-HEAD COURT-MARTIAL.

OF course the soldier who had acted as spokesman for the picket guard understood English, or he could not so readily have understood Larry's remark about going to Milan that night. The four men kept their muskets persistently pointed at our heads, as though they believed that gunpowder would not explode, or with a reckless disregard of the sanctity of human life. However, I did not consider myself in any especial peril, though I wished they would point their guns a little lower. I believed that the affair was all a mistake, which the appearance of Cuore would rectify, or which an explanation on our part would correct.

"I beg your pardon, gentlemen; but may I trouble you to land?" said the soldier in front of the others, in French, and with genuine French politeness, albeit it was utterly hollow and empty.

"Certainly," I replied. "You speak English?"

"Yes; I can speak English; but I learn from the description of two spies that one of them speaks French a little, and the other speaks it very well. You are the one who speaks it very well, I suppose," laughed the soldier, who was a sergeant.

"I contrive to make myself understood," I answered, as I stepped on shore, followed by Larry.

The soldier was so polite and considerate that I did not consider the situation as at all desperate, and I could not then classify it as one of the struggles of a soldier, though it assumed a different aspect in a short time.

"You spoke of a description, sergeant," said I, in plain English. "Do I understand you to say that you have a description of my friend and myself?"

"Yes, sir; and I must say, that you answer to the description marvellously well. Dressed in the uniform of French officers," he replied, taking a paper from his pocket, and reading therefrom. "'Brigade staff.' 'Young.' May I be allowed to inquire your ages, gentlemen?"

"I am nineteen; and this is my twin friend," laughed Larry, who seemed to consider the affair as an excellent joke.

"Thank you, gentlemen. Now, will you pardon me if I ask upon whose staff you serve?" continued the sergeant, blandly.

"Certainly; it will afford me very great pleasure to inform you that we are attached to the staff of General Eberlé, in the capacity of volunteer aids," answered Larry.

"Precisely so," exclaimed the spokesman of the soldiers, glancing at his companions, and translating the reply; and they smiled, as though the party understood the matter.

"There's no doubt about it," added Larry. "You seem to be amused."

"The description says the two Austrian spies would claim to be members of General Eberlé's staff. Will you allow me to look at your coat?" continued the sergeant, stepping up to my friend. "And yours?" he added, placing his hand upon my breast. "There it is! a hole in the coat on the left breast. I think that is sufficient. You are the gentlemen we are required to arrest."

"Probably we are," replied Larry. "You have

had it all your own way, so far. Now I will thank you to answer some of our questions. Do you know one Signor Cuore, an Italian?"

"I have not the honor," answered the sergeant.

"Have you seen an Italian with a stove-pipe hat?" asked Larry, describing our guide more fully.

"I beg your pardon, gentlemen," replied the polite sergeant; "but I am to obtain information, and not give it. I can answer no questions. It is my duty to escort you to the headquarters of our brigade."

"Right, sergeant; do your duty like a man, and stand by United Italy to the end; but you have made a mistake," continued my friend.

"Not possible, gentlemen. You answer the description perfectly."

"Where did you obtain the description?" I inquired, with great simplicity.

The sergeant only shrugged his shoulders, and made no reply. He even laughed at the folly of the question I proposed.

"What do you take us to be?" I demanded.

"Pardon, gentlemen, but we take you to be spies, in the employ of the Austrians, on your way to Milan, to inform the Austrian of the number and position of the French and Italian troops," replied the sergeant, in French.

"What does he say, Phil?"

I told my friend what the sergeant said; and certainly it was a very grave charge, considering that we were on the dividing line between the hostile armies, and on the eve of a great battle.

"Are you not satisfied, gentlemen?" inquired the bland sergeant.

"No, sir; we are not. We are what we claim to be — volunteer aids on the staff of General Eberlé. You are making a mistake in arresting us."

"There is another point in the description; and since you are not satisfied, we will proceed a little farther. I judged from your conversation that you intended to go to Milan."

"Have you seen Cuore?" asked Larry.

"I answer no questions. Will the gentlemen oblige me by showing their papers?"

"To be sure. I am willing to show all my papers; but I have nothing except some old letters, and a letter of credit," answered Larry; and he emptied his pockets.

I produced the contents of my pockets, and the

sergeant proceeded to examine my diary, which contained pockets wherein I kept my papers. One after another he opened them, and finally came to one on which the porter of the hotel in Nice had written the address of my mother's Italian friend and host at Milan.

"*Signor Bertani, Corso de Bosinare, No.* 21," continued the sergeant, reading the paper. "Do you know the gentleman whose address you have?"

"I do not," I answered.

"Did you intend to visit him in Milan?"

"I did."

"And, of course, you know that he is a traitor to his country, and a friend of the Austrians?" added the sergeant, rather warmly.

"I have been told so; but I have nothing to do with his politics. I expect to find my mother at his house in Milan."

"*Oui, oui, oui — oui — oui,*" said the soldier, shrugging his shoulders and laughing, as though he did not put implicit confidence in the truth of my statement.

"I must escort you to the headquarters of the general of brigade."

"Before you hang us, you will oblige us very

much by sending for General Eberlé," said Larry, lightly.

"We do not hang you. You shall die like soldiers — by the bullet, and not by the rope. It takes too long to hang men."

"I say, Phil, he takes a cheerful view of the subject — don't he?" said Larry, turning to me.

"I am afraid the situation is more serious than you seem to think it is," I suggested.

"How can it be serious? We can send for General Eberlé, and he will make it all right in an instant."

"Perhaps they won't take the trouble to send for him. These French officers have an ugly habit of catching a spy and hanging him without much formality," I replied. "Of course you know what a drum-head court-martial is."

"I do."

"I have heard a French officer say that ten minutes was time enough for both trial and execution."

"That would be no joke."

We walked along, side by side, with the soldiers around us in such a way that there was no chance to escape. We were conducted first to a lieutenant, who promptly ordered us to be taken to headquarters.

"I am afraid we are in a bad scrape, Larry," I said, as we marched over the unoccupied land.

"I don't think so. I tell you we are not to be hanged or shot without a hearing of some kind."

"I doubt whether they will take the trouble to inform our general of their actions."

"These men are very polite and considerate."

"But they will hang or shoot you just as quick, for all that. The man that cuts your throat will do it very politely; but he will do it none the less. I can't say that I blame these men. The case looks very strong against us. The sergeant heard you say that we intended to go to Milan, and he found the address of a traitorous Italian upon me. We were in a boat, headed towards the Austrian lines also."

"Yet the simple truth will show that we are not Austrians, or in their employ."

"Yes; if we can persuade them to believe the simple truth, which may be a very difficult matter."

"By the way, Phil, what is your opinion of Signor Cuore?"

"I presume we shall not differ in opinion just

now. But I cannot comprehend what the rascal's object is. Why should he get us into such a scrape as this?"

"I don't know; but I should like to be introduced to Signor Cuore just now," added Larry, with emphasis.

"Very likely he will appear against us."

"I don't believe he will. He evidently means to have us shot, and that our case shall be finished in short metre. Since he insisted upon my going to Milan, when I had not the least desire to go at present, I conclude that he particularly desires that I should be shot."

"Possibly he is impartial, and only desires to have us served alike."

"The villain started us in that boat alone, in order to bring about just what has happened to us."

"Undoubtedly he laid his plans very carefully. I would give something handsome to know what his motives are. I have no enemies that I know of in this part of the world."

"Are you not mixed up with those Collingsbys, your mother's brothers, and your grandfather, too?"

"I don't think they have any ill-will towards

me," I answered, giving an earnest thought to the subject.

"But, according to your own story, Phil, they believe that you are an impostor, trying to impose upon the credulity of Mrs. Farringford, a member of their family. Perhaps they are afraid that you will succeed in making that lady believe you are really her son. They hate your father, and don't choose to have anything to do with him. Isn't it likely that they have employed Signor Cuore to get rid of you in his mild and pleasant manner, that is to say, in having you hanged or shot as a spy?"

"It is possible; but the Collingsbys are very respectable people, to say the least, and I am not willing to believe that they would resort to such an infamous expedient."

"I don't know, Phil. They are respectable, as you say, and they wish to keep respectable. They believe that the Farringford blood is not respectable, and they wish to keep it at a safe distance. That's what's the matter, Phil."

"I cannot believe it."

"Your mother must have heard something about you before this time. All the Chicago Collingsbys know all about you, even to Miss Marion; and you may depend upon it, some of them have given her a hint before this time. As she must be more interested in the subject than any of the rest of them, she may have manifested a desire to inquire into the matter, which her brothers do not like. Of course they knew that you were on your way to Europe, to find your mother."

"I don't see how they should know it," I added.

"They must know it. Didn't you get a letter in Paris from Miss Marian Collingsby?"

"I did; but her father will not permit her even to speak of this subject to him."

"You are as simple-minded as an infant, Phil! Marian told her mother all about it; and she told the old man, who, while he pretended to care nothing at all about it, kept up a tremendous thinking, and privately wrote to his agents in London to look after you, and not let you see Mrs. Farringford on any account whatever. Then the London agent employed this Cuore, who was on the train with us to Paris, and has not lost sight of us since. I tell you, Phil, that little scene in the garden of the Tuileries was got up by him merely to make our acquaintance, and secure our confidence by doing us a favor. It is just as clear as dock mud to me, Phil."

"I don't say that you are wrong, Larry; but if your theory is correct, why was the villain so particular that you should go to Milan, and be sacrificed with me?"

"That may look like a stumper to you, but I can explain it to my own satisfaction. This fellow knows that I am a particular friend of yours, and he knows very well, if you disappeared, that I should find you if I had to explore the continent to do so. He knows very well that I should find him, too. I think the villain understands me first rate, and believes that it would not be a prudent step to separate us. I'm right, Phil."

"I don't know that it makes much difference whether you are right or wrong, now, Larry. We are in a bad scrape."

"But we shall get out of it, and give Cuore a chance to try the game over again. I should like to put my paws upon him."

"He will keep out of the way as long as he can. Here is the line of the camps, and we shall soon know what is to become of us."

We were conducted to the headquarters of the

general of brigade, where the sergeant reported his prisoners, and asked for orders. After waiting half an hour, several officers appeared, but there was no general of brigade among them. They seated themselves on camp-stools, and strangely enough, a drum lay on the ground near them, though I am sure it had not been placed there with any reference to the present proceedings. It was an ominous emblem to me, and I did not like the appearance of it. I was unable to determine whether the officers before us constituted a court-martial or not, for I could not hear any of the proceedings. Larry was called up first, and one of the officers proceeded to question him in French. He could not even understand the questions that were put to him. Then one of them addressed him in German; and Larry answered, "*Nix.*" The sergeant suggested that the other prisoner spoke French, and I was called up.

It appeared that the sergeant and his fellow-soldiers had already told their story, and that we were really condemned already. I was asked to explain my relations with Signor Bertani, and how I happened to be on my way to Milan in the uniform of a French officer. Before I said anything, I produced my passport, which I had stitched into my coat for safety.

"You are an American?" said one of the officers, exhibiting much surprise, as he examined this important paper.

"I am."

"Good on your head, Phil! You have hit the nail in the right place this time," exclaimed Larry.

CHAPTER XVII.

IN WHICH PHIL AND LARRY ARE SAVED FROM A HARD FATE BY A MOVEMENT OF THE BRIGADE.

"IF you are an American, how do you happen to be in the army of France?" asked the officer, who appeared to be the highest in rank, and who was doubtless the president of the court-martial, if it was such.

"We are both volunteer aids-de-camp, on the staff of General Eberlé," I replied.

"Is it possible?" added the officer, glancing at his companions.

They looked at one another, and then examined my passport again, whose signature and broad seal could not be ignored. Then they began to puzzle themselves over the personal description, and I saw that one of them could read English. The comparison could not but be satisfactory, for the shape of my chin and the color of my eyes were correctly given, as well as the other details.

"Is your friend an American also?" asked the officer.

"He was born in England, but has lived in America from his childhood," I answered, believing that the simple truth is always better than falsehood and deception.

One of the officers walked up to Larry, and spoke to him in German; but of course neither he nor I understood a word that was said.

"*Nix*," replied Larry, shrugging his shoulders.

The speaker then explained that he had told my friend he might depart in peace. Such a permission, if he had understood it, would have surprised him into a word or a look that might have betrayed him; but Larry made no sign that could excite a suspicion.

"Has your friend a passport?" asked the chief officer, turning to me again.

"He has not," I replied. "He left New York rather suddenly, and did not think to procure a passport, as one has but little need of it now."

"But you were going to Milan?" said the officer, returning to the suspicious side of the question.

"I wished to go to Milan because my mother is there."

The military gentleman shrugged his shoulders, and was evidently incredulous.

"And you have the address of Signor Bertani, who is an Italian, but in the employ of the Austrians. No, no, no!"

"My mother is his guest," I added.

"No, no!"

"I speak only the truth."

"Humph — possibly."

"We have already declared that we were attached to the staff of General Eberlé. If you have any doubt in regard to the truth of what we say, you can refer to that distinguished officer," I suggested.

"General Eberlé is seven or eight kilomètres distant. You refer to some one who is conveniently removed from us. We make short work with spies," continued the officer. "We may be ordered to march in half an hour, and we have no time to waste upon persons taken in the very act of entering the enemy's lines. We have good evidence that you are spies."

"You refer to Signor Cuore, who is a spy himself," I answered, with some spirit. "He has a pass in German for three persons to go through the Austrian lines."

The officers looked at each other and smiled.

"For two persons," said the officer, correcting me.

"He told us it was for three. Neither of us can speak or read German."

"Here is the pass," added the speaker, taking from his pocket the paper which Cuore had exhibited, and showing it to me.

Giving the pass to the gentleman who read and spoke German, he desired him to translate it to us. He gave me the contents of the paper in French. It was an order requiring picket guards and sentinels to pass Philip Farringford and Lawrence Grimsby through the Austrian lines, and to give them every facility for reaching the general in command at Milan. I told Larry in English what the pass was, and we both understood why Cuore had declined to have the Swiss orderly read it. Of course the paper was a forgery; but we were utterly incapable of fathoming the ultimate purpose of Cuore in leading us into this trap. As the officer seemed to be very patient, in spite of his declaration that he had no time to waste upon such persons as we appeared to be, I began to explain our relations with General Eberlé and with

Cuore. The party listened attentively, and permitted me to finish my narrative. I doubt not I made some blunders in the use of the French language, for several times I was called upon to repeat what I had said. When I had concluded my story, there was a general shrugging of shoulders, and a general smile of incredulity.

It was now nearly dark, and the officers, after consulting together for a moment, seated themselves on camp-stools around the drum which I had before observed. Larry and myself were ordered to stand at an opening in the ring opposite the officer who had questioned us. I concluded that the formal proceedings were about to commence.

"It looks serious, Larry," I said.

"That's so; but you mustn't give it up, Phil. Make a spread-eagle speech. If I could speak the language, I would do so. Shake your passport at them."

"I am afraid it will do no good."

"Try it, and see. I have no idea of being shot in this way by these frog-eaters, when I stand ready to fight for them. It isn't giving a fellow a fair show."

"Have you anything to say why you should not be shot as spies?" said the president of the court-martial.

"We demand a fair trial," I replied. "We are Americans, and we are in the service of France, ready to fight her battles. We are not spies, and we ask for the advice and assistance of the nearest representative of the United States government. We also demand the privilege of confronting our accuser. He is a villain and a liar."

I spoke with energy; and, adopting the suggestion of Larry, I flourished my passport with vigor in the face of the presiding officer.

"You wish to see Signor Cuore?" added the president.

"We do."

"Bring Signor Cuore."

The proceedings were suspended; but some time elapsed before the Italian was produced. I saw by his actions that he came very unwillingly. He was placed by the side of the drum in the centre of the circle, and required to state what he knew about us. He declared that he had followed us from Paris, where he had seen us in communication with several Austrians, and that he had watched us up to the moment we had attempted to pass the river, when he deemed it his duty to inform the picket-guard of our intentions, which he had done.

"Where did you get the pass which you allege is ours?" I asked.

"I found it where you lost it," replied Cuore, chuckling as though he had done a clever thing.

"Where did you find it?" I demanded, energetically.

"You dropped it when you pulled out your handkerchief."

"You do not say where you found it."

"On the bank of the canal, before you got into the boat."

"Were you with us at the time?"

"No; I was behind you."

"But not in company with us?"

"No, certainly not."

"Were you at the camp of General Eberlé with us?"

"No; never."

"Did you not come down from the camp of General Eberlé to the canal?"

"I did not."

"All right, my boy! If the Evil One should look for a liar, where in all Italy could we put you?" added Larry, who had listened attentively to the conversation, which was carried on in English.

"He would take you, and not look any farther," replied Cuore.

"What are you saying?" demanded the president, impatiently, for he did not understand English.

I related the substance of the conversation in French, and Cuore indorsed my version as correct.

"Now, *Monsieur le Chef de Bataillon*," I continued, guessing at the rank of the officer, "this man says he was not with us at the camp of General Eberlé, or at any other time."

"Certainly not," added Cuore.

"If you would do me the favor to send for the officer of the guard at the next post, he will tell you that we passed this Italian through his lines."

"He only wants to gain time," replied Cuore, with one of his politest bows.

"I have not time to send to any post."

"Will you condemn two innocent men — Americans?" I pleaded.

THE COURT-MARTIAL. Page 238.

"The evidence is very full and satisfactory."

"But this man is a liar. He showed this pass at the camp of our general."

"No. All that he said proves to be true. We found the address of Signor Bertani upon you. If you are in the French service, you are deserters; if not, you are spies, for you were trying to pass our lines, and spoke of going to Milan, but not to-night. It is a plain case. Gentlemen, give me your attention," said the officer, addressing his companions.

Just at this moment the tap of a drum and the heavy tramp of a considerable body of men were heard in the area between the line and the river. They attracted the attention of all the party. An officer with hasty step walked up to the members of the court-martial, and asked for the general of brigade in command.

"Good! Monsieur Foucault!" shouted Larry, at the top of his lungs.

"Ah, Monsieur Grimsby!" exclaimed the officer, walking up to my friend and grasping his hand.

"Where is General Eberlé?" asked Larry.

"Our brigade is ordered to bivouac here, near the river. Give us joy! We shall be in the fight.

But, pardon, I have an order to deliver to the general of brigade at this point."

" Pardon, also. We are in trouble, and if you don't get us out of the scrape, we shall be shot as spies in five minutes more."

" Impossible ! "

" Fact, my boy ! Speak a good word for us, and it will be all right."

" Messieurs, these gentlemen are my comrades on the staff of General Eberlé."

" Is it possible ? " exclaimed the principal officer, as though it was an entirely new idea to him.

" You can bet high on it," added Larry, whose French ear was improving wonderfully.

Suddenly my friend sprang away from me, and I saw him pounce upon the lying Italian, who, seeing that the current had turned in our favor, was trying to sneak away.

" No, you don't, my fair child of Italy ! " cried Larry, as he dragged Cuore into the ring. " You have got up a little entertainment here for somebody, and you must stay and face the music."

" You will oblige me by detaining that man," said Lieutenant Foucault. " He has been hanging around our camp for several days. These gentlemen are particular friends of our *chef de brigade*, and any favor accorded to them will be a service rendered to him."

"Arrest the Italian!" said the president to the men who had guarded Larry and myself.

In a moment Cuore had a soldier on each side of him.

"*Je demande pardon*," continued the officer, extending his hand to me. "I have made a great mistake."

"I think you are rather summary in your proceedings; for, if I understand the situation, you were about to sentence us to be shot."

"But the proof was very strong," pleaded he.

"There was no evidence that we were spies; and you refused to inform General Eberlé of our situation. But you were only too zealous in the discharge of your duty," I replied.

The aid found the general of the brigade, and delivered his message. Several officers congratulated us upon our fortunate escape, and we were permitted to depart. But we were not ready yet to go. Larry insisted that he had "a bone to pick" with Cuore. It was plainly the purpose of this man to sacrifice us. He wanted our lives, and had actually laid a snare, by which we were to be shot as spies. I could not fathom his purpose; and Larry was equally unable to do so.

"Will you go with me to headquarters?" asked Foucault, when he had delivered his message.

"Not yet," replied Larry, "unless you can take this Italian with you."

"Very likely I can."

"He arrived in the camp from Milan this morning, and if there are any spies around here, in my opinion he is one of them. General Eberlé would have ordered his arrest this morning if he had not considered him our friend."

"I will speak with the *chef de bataillon*," replied the aid, walking towards that officer.

A short consultation resulted in an order for the soldiers to conduct Cuore to the headquarters of General Eberlé. We followed him, and found our brigade quartered not far from the canal where we had been arrested. The general had just completed the disposition of his force when we arrived. He gazed at us with astonishment, and with no less surprise at Cuore under guard. As briefly as possible we told him what had occurred.

"The man is a villain!" exclaimed the general.

"Italy's skies never glowed over a greater villain!" added Larry.

"Why does he seek your lives?"

"No Italian sage is wise enough to know. Being Yankees, we can guess; being philosophers,— a least, Phil is philosophical,— we desire to investigate."

"I shall hold him as a spy, for he says he came from Milan, and is a native of that city," replied General Eberlé, readily comprehending our wishes. "We will have him searched, and you shall examine his papers, if you wish."

"We do wish; but first, we should like to question him," replied Phil.

We seated ourselves upon camp-stools, and the guards were ordered to bring up the culprit.

CHAPTER XVIII.

IN WHICH PHIL AND LARRY SOLVE A PROBLEM, AND THE ITALIAN MAKES A BAD MOVE.

"I DON'T understand it at all," said I, while we were waiting for the guards to bring up the prisoner. "I can't fathom the motives of this miserable Italian; and the more I think of it, the more confused I become."

"My brains are all boggled up over the matter," added Larry; "but the only thing I can make of it is, that he is an agent of those Farringfords, of Chicago. You are a good-looking fellow, Phil, but they evidently don't mean to have you come into their family."

"Possibly he is what you say," I replied, musing again on the subject, though I thought the Farringfords were altogether too dignified to resort to such trickery.

"What can we do with this fellow, general?"

asked Larry, appealing to our powerful military friend.

"Do anything what you please with ze man," replied the general. "He have said he has been in Milan. I take him for a spy from ze Austrians."

"You have him on the hip, then," laughed my friend.

"On ze hip?"

"Where the hair is short."

"Ze hair?"

"In a tight place, I mean."

"What is that?" asked the bewildered Frenchman.

"No gentleman ought to be expected to understand such slang," I interposed.

"I have thought I know ze English language," added the general, shrugging his shoulders.

"But these are idioms," laughed Larry.

"No, they are not; they are only slang expressions. My friend means that you have the advantage of this Italian," I explained.

"I have ze advantage?"

"Why don't you speak English to him, Phil? 'On the hip' is a clearer expression than having the advantage. At any rate, you have the advantage of the general, for he don't know what you mean any better than he did what I meant."

"He intended to say that you have Cuore where you can do as you please with him," I added to the general.

"*Oui, oui, oui — oui — oui!*" exclaimed the general, after the manner of his countrymen when an obscure idea becomes plain to them. "I can put him on ze hip, with a handkerchief over his eyes, with a file of soldiers before him, who shall fire at him till he die."

"Don't do that just yet, general, if you please," interposed Larry. "That would be putting him on the hip rather too much."

"I shall do what you wish. You are ze court-martial. You shall try ze prisoner. You shall say if he is guilty or not guilty; and you shall say if he shall be shot, if he shall be hanged, if he shall live. He have come," said General Eberlé, as the soldiers appeared, conducting the prisoner into our presence.

"This way, my brave son of United Italy," shouted Larry; and the soldiers brought the Italian to the place where we were seated.

"You have sent for me, and I have come,"

said Cuore, trying to put a bold face upon the matter.

"You stole that remark from a play; it is no more original than your rascality. Are you going to Milan to-night, as you promised, Signor Cuore?"

"I am not in condition to go now," replied he, glancing at his guards.

"It seems you had no intention of going to Milan. When were you there last?"

Cuore looked at the general, and then at Larry, and evidently did not deem it prudent to answer this question.

"You have said you were in Milan last night," added the general, sternly.

"I was not there last night," answered Cuore.

"You have lied, then. These gentlemen have said what you told them. I shall take ze word of ze gentlemen. I shall treat you like a spy."

"I am not a spy, general," protested the Italian, startled by this declaration.

"You said you were in the secret service. Who employs you?" asked General Eberlé, in French.

"I am in the service of the police department," answered Cuore.

"Have you been in Milan?"

"No, general."

"What is your business with these gentlemen?"

"I only desire to assist them."

"And for that reason you denounced us as spies," I interposed.

"That was your own fault," replied the villain, coolly. "I only desired to serve you; and I expected, when I had taken you to your mother, that you would reward me handsomely for my trouble. That is the whole of it. I was only anxious to make some money."

"Did you expect to make any money by denouncing us as spies?" I demanded in English, for the accommodation of Larry.

"You denounced yourselves. You were foolish enough to talk about going to Milan while you were in the boat, which was the same thing as telling the soldiers on picket that you intended to go there."

"Why didn't you return to us, as you promised?" asked Larry.

"I could not. The soldiers arrested me. I told them you were officers, fishing; and if you had not spoken of going to Milan, it would have been all right. After you were arrested, I was obliged to tell the whole truth, or I should have been shot at once."

"Liar that thou art!" cried Larry. "When did you write that German pass?"

The scoundrel had evidently forgotten about the pass, which fully proved that he had prepared his plan for sacrificing us long before we left the camp.

We all questioned him for some time, and the more he said the deeper he involved himself in the tangle of falsehood and deceit.

"Cuore, this is all bosh," said Larry, when our patience was exhausted. "We are satisfied that you are here for a purpose, and that your purpose is to make an end of Phil and myself."

"Nothing of the kind, gentlemen. You wrong me. I have been your friend. I have done all I could to serve you. I saved you from the police in Paris, I assisted you in the steamers, and have done everything to aid you. You could not have reached Italy without my help."

"But you brought us here to have us shot by order of a court-martial. Do you know a family of the name of Farringford?" added Larry, sharply.

"I know our friend here, but no other one of the name," replied Cuore, shaking his head.

"Who employed you to take charge of us? In whose employ do you labor to have us shot, drowned, or otherwise disposed of?"

"You wrong me, gentlemen."

"General, will you do us the favor to have this man searched?" added Larry, turning to our military friend.

"Certainly," replied he, giving the order in French to the sergeant in charge of the prisoner.

The conspirator evidently did not relish this measure, for he turned pale, and I saw that he was very much agitated. The sergeant obeyed the order, and searched the prisoner in the most thorough manner. A considerable sum of money in napoleons was found in his purse, and several letters and papers. The sergeant was directed to return the purse, but the papers were handed to me for examination.

"Those are my private papers," said Cuore.

"Precisely so; and that is the particular reason why we wish to see them," answered Larry.

"I took you to be gentlemen," added the prisoner, faintly.

"We are very much obliged to you for the compliment your good judgment paid to us, and we are very sorry to be obliged to consult your private papers before we venture an opinion upon you. Open the documents, Phil."

"I protest! This is an outrage," said Cuore, warming up.

"Right! Go on with the outrage, Phil."

I opened a letter, which was in Italian, and I could not read it. I handed it to General Eberlé.

"I am in the employ of the police department of Paris, and you have no right to examine my papers," continued the prisoner. "It is an outrage."

"Proceed with the outrage, Phil," added Larry, as I picked up a letter which bore the London postmark.

It was directed to Cuore at Marseilles. I opened it, and found it was in English. I looked for the signature first, but there was none. This fact was an indication that the fellow was in the employ of some one who would not even trust his name to paper. I did not recognize the handwriting, as I should have done if it had been that of either of the Farringfords of Chicago. The letter had contained a circular note for one thousand francs, and promised further remittances as the business proceeded. The other letters and papers were of no consequence to us, and our search seemed to amount to nothing, notwithstanding the violent objections of Cuore. We concluded that we had not found his most important documents; but the most diligent search failed to reveal anything further upon his person.

"Who wrote this letter?" I asked, holding the one from London.

"I decline to answer," replied Cuore, who seemed to be greatly reassured by the ill success of our inquiries.

"Never mind, my sunny son of Italy. We have another string to our bow," said Larry.

"What is that?" I asked.

"General, has the mail-bag gone?" inquired Larry.

"No. We were ordered to march a few moments after you left," replied the general.

"Good! Our friend here mailed some letters. I think we had better examine them."

The general summoned his orderly, and directed the mail-bag to be brought to him. I kept my eye on the prisoner, who became very much agitated again as soon as he understood our purpose. The small leather bag, in which the letters of the brigade were sent to the nearest postoffice, was soon brought to the general, who opened it.

"Sir Philip Grimsby," said he, reading the superscription of the first he took out.

"That's mine," added Larry.

"Miss Ella Gracewood."

"That's mine," I replied.

"Miss Blanche Fennimore."

"All right," said Larry.

Half a dozen more to people in Paris and other parts of France followed.

"Here is another Grimsby," added the general. "Mr. Miles Grimsby."

"That's more to the point. Let us see it. He is a cousin of mine."

Larry took the letter, and the address suggested a now theory to me, as it must have done to my friend.

"That's not my writing," said Larry.

"Nor mine," I added. "No one here but ourselves can possibly know Miles Grimsby."

"Doubted!" exclaimed Larry. "I begin to see through the hole in this millstone."

"So do I."

"What you have discovered?" asked the general, with interest.

"We should like very much to know what is in this letter," replied Larry.

"The letter is sealed," said the general, doubtfully.

"But it was written by Cuore to the man who employed him to see that we do not return to England."

"It is not my letter; I know nothing about it," interposed the prisoner, struggling to appear indifferent, in which he signally failed.

"If it is not your letter, of course it does not concern you," added Larry.

"No; but you have no right to open any person's letter. As an agent of the police, I will inform against you if you open a single envelope."

"Martial law here," said the general, taking the letter into his own hands. "You do not open ze letter, Monsieur Greemsby; you do not open ze letter, Monsieur Farringfor'. Ze general open ze letter. I take ze responsibility. You have understood me?"

"Perfectly," we both replied.

"And you, Signor Cuore?"

"I protest! No one but the members of the police have the right to open a letter," replied the prisoner, much alarmed.

"You protest, and I open ze letter," said the general, suiting the action to the word. "*Voilà!*" exclaimed the general, pointing to the signature of the letter, as he handed it to Larry. "You have wrote ze letter, signore. It have your name with ze pen at ze end of it."

"This is entirely to the point, Phil," said Larry, as he glanced at the sheet. "The next time you see a Farringford, apologize to the whole race of them for the injury I have done them. This fellow is not working up your case, but mine."

"This is an outrage," said Cuore, angrily.

"So it is, my precious scoundrel; but by just such outrages as this is innocence like mine protected from villany like yours."

At this moment, Cuore, hopeless now that any cunning or any accident could conceal his rascality, sprang away from the guards who were standing on each side of him, and leaped upon Larry, who held the important letter in his hand. But the sergeant was hardly less active, and threw himself upon his prisoner, followed by three soldiers. The Italian struggled to shake off his persecutors. The peril of his situation has rendered him desperate, and before the sergeant and his companions could obtain a firm hold of him, he darted out from under them. In another instant he was running with all his might towards the pickets on the bank of the river. The soldiers grasped their muskets and pursued him. Three shots followed each other in rapid succession, after we lost sight of the party in the darkness.

"I don't believe that fellow will trouble us any more," said Larry, after we heard the report of the muskets.

"I have no wish to have him shot," I replied.

"Nor I; but he has brought it upon himself. Here they come. They have finished him."

The soldiers returned, bringing with them the Italian. He was not dead, and I raised the lantern from the camp-stool to ascertain his condition. The surgeon was at hand, and soon ascertained that two bullets had passed through the body of Cuore. His case was doubtful, but not hopeless, and he was sent to the rear.

By the light of the lantern we read his letter to Miles Grimsby, in which he reported progress to his employer. He said that his "friends" intended to start for Milan, and he was "afraid" some accident would happen to them.

CHAPTER XIX.

IN WHICH PHIL INVENTS AND LAUNCHES AN AQUATIC MACHINE, AND PREPARES TO CROSS THE TICINO.

IT had never occurred either to Larry or myself that Cuore had any connection with the Grimsbys. It is true that Miles had solemnly warned my friend of the peril he incurred by allowing events to take their natural course — by permitting Sir Philip to have his own way. Neither of us gave the baronet's grandson the credit of being a person of any particular force of character, either for good or evil. We regarded his warning as an idle threat, intended to intimidate a weak mind, but to have no effect whatever upon such minds as we flattered ourselves that we possessed.

"Miles has some grit in his constitution," said Larry, after the soldiers had borne the wounded Italian to the rear. "I would not have believed that he had the spunk to kill a flea, or raise his hand against a good-sized bull-frog."

"It does not require much courage to employ an Italian bravo to do your dirty work for you," I replied.

"It was very well managed, whoever did it; and, so far as I can see, the plot would have been successful if General Eberlé's brigade had not moved over here at just this time."

"Probably it would have been successful. I can't say I like the way these Frenchmen do these things. Sometimes they shoot a man, and hear the evidence for or against him afterwards. We came within one of being shot on the testimony of this miserable Cuore."

"Precisely so; and I judge, from the stories of those who speak English, that many a fellow as good-looking as you or I has been shot on no better evidence. There's a great deal of uncertainty in this world, Phil," added my companion, sagely.

"In this particular part of it, and at this particular time, there is; and this fact convinces me that we are out of our element. If I had known no more French than you do, Larry, we should have been sacrificed before our brigade arrived."

"Correct; and, Phil, we will get out of this scrape as soon as convenient; for, however I may feel in regard to myself, I will not risk your neck among the Philistines any longer than is absolutely necessary."

"I am afraid that you are in greater danger than I am, Larry," I answered.

"Why so!"

"Because Miles Grimsby will never be satisfied till he has removed you from between himself and his expectations."

"Now that I understand the matter, I don't care a fig for him. Miles will find it a very difficult thing to wipe me out."

"He has exhibited no little tact in managing his case so far. He went down to London with us, and there employed this reckless Italian to follow us."

"Of course that little farce in the gardens of the Tuileries was only a trick of Cuore to introduce himself," added Larry.

"That's all; but I have no doubt that he is, or has been, in the employ of the police department, as a spy, a shadow, a stool-pigeon."

"But I wonder where Miles found him."

Miles has travelled on the continent, and very likely Cuore has been a *courrier* or *valet de place*, employed by him."

"If he gets well, very likely we shall have to fight this battle over again in some other form. No matter; it will make it lively for me."

By this time the troops of the brigade were asleep on the ground, where they had bivouacked for the night. It was said in the camp that McMahon, with the Imperial Guard, had been moving towards the north, and it was believed that the great battle was close at hand. It seemed to me then that I was quite willing to avoid the savage contest, in which I had no particular interest; but I saw no way to do so. We had been praised and flattered by the officers, called the "brave Americans," and we felt that much was expected of us. At any rate, we were too deeply committed by our pride and self-respect to run away. We drew our blankets over us, and went to sleep together on the right bank of the Ticino, near what is now historic ground.

Early the next morning, though the sound of booming guns came not to our waiting ears, and all was as still as if earth knew no discordant notes, our brigade was in marching order. Haversacks were filled with rations, ammunition was served out, and every preparation was made for active operations.

On that day was fought the great and decisive battle of Magenta.

Its story is briefly told. On the left of the allied army, McMahon had marched, two days before, to the north. On the preceding day this force had crossed the Ticino at Turbigo, a considerable distance above the spot where the Austrians had evidently expected the attack. But the enemy hurried forward his troops in that direction, and soon had a superior force between McMahon and the main body of the allies. On the day of the battle, the emperor crossed the bridge at Buffalora, and took position in front of one hundred and twenty-five thousand Austrians, who, apparently unable to determine the plan of the allies, made no attack until about noon. Guyulai, the Austrian commander-in-chief, learning that the bridge of Buffalora had been captured, and that the invaders had crossed the river, despatched a force to drive back the allies, and retake the bridge. Canrobert was to have followed the emperor, who had advanced with the grenadiers of the Imperial Guard, but was delayed, and for a time the situation of the emperor was critical. The Guard stood their ground with a steadiness which has hardly a parallel in history. Seven times in the course of two hours did the enemy charge upon the little force which surrounded his majesty, but were as often repulsed. Then the Guard, weary and impatient under this passive fighting, attacked the Austrians. Canrobert then appeared, and the position was won.

During these critical moments, when the Imperial Guard were almost borne under by the force of opposing numbers, the emperor was frequently observed to cast his eyes anxiously in the direction of Turbigo, from which he expected the force of McMahon to come. It came at last, having fought its way through a superior force, and the junction was effected in accordance with the plan of the emperor. But the Austrians fought bravely to the last, and were slowly driven back upon Magenta, which was taken, house by house, by the French, and the great victory was complete and final.

Until late in the afternoon, our brigade had

been wholly unoccupied, except in watching the movements of the enemy on the other side of the river. We were part of the force on the right of the emperor, whose duty it was to prevent the enemy from crossing the river, and taking the allies on the flank. An Austrian *corps d'armée* was stationed at Abbiate Grasso, directly in front of our position, which we were either to neutralize or follow, as the case might require.

At noon we heard the roar of the guns, and the sharp rattle of the musketry at Buffalora. The combat deepened as the day advanced. From the highest points of observation, even from the tops of the trees and the roofs of the houses, the glasses of the field officers were directed towards the country between Abbiate Grasso and Magenta, to obtain the earliest intelligence of the movements of the enemy in front of our division. A pontoon train was in readiness to throw a bridge over the river, whenever the situation required an advance. But the other side of the river was still picketed by the Austrians. General Eberlé was constantly in consultation with the general of division, and they were evidently much perplexed to ascertain the operations of the Austrian corps in front of them.

To my surprise, I found myself quite as much excited as the Frenchmen around me, while Larry was almost wild with the desire to take a more active part in the great events of the day. We were both mounted, and had done our full share of duty. The troops were kept in line, in readiness to move; but we all agreed that we had a very stupid part to perform.

"Dull music, Phil," said my friend.

"Rather; but I suppose we shall soon have something to do," I answered.

"I am afraid not."

"Of course, if the French carry the day above, the Austrians will not long remain in front of us. As soon as they move, we shall cross over and take the Austrians on the left."

"Do you know, Phil, I believe those Dutchmen over there are fooling our generals?"

"What makes you think so?"

"We can't see through all those trees. A hundred thousand men could move beyond the slope without being seen. If I were the general of division here, I would cross the river this instant," replied Larry, highly excited.

"Don't you see that battery over there?"

"Hang the battery! It has only a dozen guns or so. That must be carried as soon as we cross."

"But it makes a difference whether or not it is supported by a *corps d'armée*. Our generals ought to have some one on the other side of the river, to let them know how the thing is going there," I suggested.

"Suppose you go over, Phil?" laughed Larry.

"I am entirely willing," I replied, hardly thinking what I was saying.

"I should like to go with you, if the thing were possible," added my friend.

"It is possible, of course."

"What, with pickets on the other side of the stream? I think not."

"But it is possible, and I will agree to do it."

"I will go with you, Phil; but it can't be done. You would be shot twenty times before you could get over. Here is the general," added Larry, as a party of field officers passed near us.

Larry told our general what I had said.

"Not possible!" exclaimed he.

"I think it is; and I will undertake the job, if you will support me," I answered, with a recklessness which has ever since amazed me.

" I will give you ze support of ze whole brigage, with grand pleasure," said the general. " We want ze information. Suppose ze enemy move; we don't see him; we don't know when he go; we don't know where he go; no !"

" I will be over there in half an hour, or an hour, at most, if you will do what I ask."

" Certainly, I do all you ask," added the general, with enthusiasm.

" You have a battery of artillery. Drive the pickets back from the river with it."

" Yes."

" And give me one of the large copper soup-boilers from the cuisine," I added.

" A soup-kettle ! " exclaimed the military gentleman. " Will you cross in a soup-kettle ? Ze Austrians will make a riddle of you with bullets."

" I do not purpose to cross *in* the soup-boiler. But if you will leave that part to me, I will manage it."

" As you please."

" Do you see that tall tree on the top of the little hill ? " I asked, pointing to a very tall poplar, whose branches had been trimmed off for seventy or eighty feet from the ground, as they are often seen in France and Italy.

"I see him," replied General Eberlé, nervously.

"If the Austrians have marched towards Magenta, I will wave my handkerchief from the top of that tree, or some other one near it."

"Bravo!" shouted the general, hugging me in his enthusiasm, as though I had already done all I promised to do.

"Now send the soup-boiler down to the canal," I replied, pointing to the willows where we had embarked the evening before.

"Can't I go with you, Phil?" asked Larry, as we walked to our baggage-wagon.

"Only one can go."

"But you will be shot, Phil."

"I think not. I'm going in for a safe job. You shall help me off."

I threw off my uniform, and put on a pair of plain pants, which, with a shirt and a pair of shoes, was my entire suit. Taking a saw, a hatchet, some rope, and nails, I hastened to the canal, attended by Larry. I found a joist which had belonged to a bridge that had been destroyed, from which I cut off two pieces three feet in length. Placing them two feet apart, I nailed two sticks securely across them, so as to keep them in position, forming a frame three feet by two. By this time the soup-kettle had arrived. Putting the frame in the water, I placed the boiler upon it, upside down, to ascertain if the joists would float it.

The experiment was not satisfactory, and I was obliged to add two more sticks, in order to increase the floatage power of the raft. It was a success this time; and turning over the boiler, I lashed it firmly to the sticks.

"What under the light of the blue canopy are you doing, Phil?" demanded Larry, who had watched me with interest, and assisted me as I required. "What sort of a machine do you call that?"

"I don't call it. Now lend me your revolver."

I took the pistol, and fired six shots at the copper, which only dented it, and none of the balls went through.

"All right, Larry. You see it is bullet-proof."

"I see it is; the metal gives so that the shots bound off."

"Now help me put it into the water."

We launched the novel machine, and I found that the floatage of the wood was none too great, for the raft was very nearly submerged by the weight upon it. We towed the thing down to the mouth of the canal.

"Now, Larry, go and tell the general to clean out the pickets," I continued.

"All right; but what are you going to do?"

"I'm going to swim across the river, with my head raised up in the boiler."

"You will smother."

"No; the top is just above the surface of the water. But I can tip it a little when I need ventilation."

But at that moment a bullet whistled unpleasantly near my head, and I "ducked" under the bank of the canal. It was fired by the pickets on the other side. Phil left me, and in a few moments I saw the French battery dashing towards the river.

CHAPTER XX.

IN WHICH PHIL AND LARRY TAKE PART IN THE BATTLE OF MAGENTA, AND VISIT MILAN.

AS soon as Larry had started the battery towards the river, he returned to the canal to assist me in moving off my aquatic machine. Before he joined me, the French cannon were waking up the Austrians on the other side. From the earth-works opposite a sharp fire was opened. A company of French riflemen swept the bank of the river at the same time, and the place was altogether too hot for the pickets. I saw them retreating from the shelter of the willows near the river, and the way was thus prepared for my attempt.

"I am all ready, Larry," said I. "The coast is as clear as it will be."

"I'm afraid those Dutchmen will gobble you up as soon as you land," he replied, anxiously.

18

"No, I think not. At any rate, I shall do the best I can to keep out of their way."

"But I must go over and take care of you."

"Don't you think I can take care of myself?"

"I doubt it."

"I have seen more of this sort of thing than you have, Larry, and, now I am in it, I feel quite at home."

"That Indian skirmishing again!" laughed he.

"It was hotter than anything we have seen here yet."

"Perhaps it was. But I must go with you, Phil."

"No, you stay here. I should have to take care of you besides myself, if you went."

"Good, Phil! The lamb is becoming a lion; but I am a first-class tiger, and I feel moved to go with you. I should never forgive myself if you should be killed instead of me. You have a mother—"

"And you have a grandfather," I interposed, as I prepared to put my head inside of the soup-boiler.

"Never mind him. One good turn deserves another, and I shall leave him to take care of himself, as he did me."

"I dare say your 'taking off' would oblige your cousin Miles very much."

"I'm not going to be taken off to oblige him. There is room for two heads in that big kettle."

"Room for the heads, but not for the shoulders under them. I have to swim, Larry, and two of us could do nothing in such close quarters. Besides, my dear fellow, I want you to stay on the shore here, and see that nothing goes wrong with me. Keep out of sight, and make no sign, or you will betray me. If you see any chance to help me, do so; but remember that discretion is the better part of valor in a situation like this."

"Good by, Phil, if we never meet again, for you are going into the lion's den, and he will bite your head off, all because I am not with you to take care of you. I didn't think you could be so obstinate."

"Adieu for the present, Larry. Keep your eye on me as long as you can, but don't show yourself."

I lay down in the water, and raised my head under the soup-kettle. The water was about up to my middle, and I was obliged to stoop under my armor. The rim of the boiler was not an inch above the surface of the water, but this space was enough to afford me a supply of air, and to enable me to see my course over the stream. Grasping the frame on which my head-armor rested, I pushed off. The depth of the river gradually increased as I advanced, and I was soon obliged to swim. As there was little or no current, I had no difficulty in propelling the machine; but I was careful to make no swash in the water that would attract the attention of the enemy. My hands were placed on one of the boards I had nailed across the joists; and I found that my weight quite submerged the boiler in front of me, so that I could not see ahead; but the part behind me was above the water, so that I did not want for air.

"Starboard!" said Larry, in a voice loud enough for me to hear.

Shifting my weight to the after part of the machine, so as to permit the kettle to rise in front of me, I saw that I was headed directly down the stream, towards the battery, which was belching forth fire, smoke, and grape-shot. Changing my course, I propelled the machine with my feet. The river was not wide, and in a few moments I found I could touch bottom with my feet. Thus far not a shot from the shore had struck the kettle, and I concluded that the enemy had been so much occupied with the battery as not to notice me. Wading slowly in towards the Lombardian shore, I crowded my machine in among the willows which covered the bank. Resting from my violent exertions, — for I had worked hard in propelling the huge boiler over the river, — I listened attentively for any sounds that denoted the near presence of the Austrians. I could hear nothing but the roar of the artillery, still engaged in the duel across the stream, and I ventured to crawl out from beneath my armor.

Keeping my head behind the kettle, I attempted to peer through the willows. I could see nothing of the enemy in this direction, though an occasional shell exploded just below me, and I could hear the rattle of grape-shot among the trees, between me and the earth-works. While I was thus examining the ground over which I wished to advance, I heard a noise in the water, which caused me to turn around. There in the river, and half way across, was Larry, swimming lustily towards me, without the shelter of a soup-boiler, or any other protective apparatus. For an instant I trembled for him; but when I considered that not a shot had been fired at the moving boiler, and that the pickets had been driven back by the fire of the artillery, I could hardly keep from laughing at the pains I had taken to secure a safe passage. With strong and lusty strokes Larry rapidly approached me, and was soon within easy speaking distance of me.

" What are you about, Larry ? " I asked, when he ceased to swim, and began to wade towards me.

" About my own business and that of the French army," replied he, puffing with his exertions.

" Are you mad ? "

" Never was in better humor in my life."

" Duck under, Larry, or some of the Austrians will see you," I called, earnestly.

" Don't be alarmed, Phil. I helped to put a head on you, and I have no notion of losing my own. There isn't an Austrian within a quarter of a mile of you," he answered, walking erect in the water towards me. " But why stand ye here all the day idle ? "

" I was just feeling my way up to the shore. I am provoked with you, Larry. Why did you come over ? "

" My conscience reproached me for permitting a youth like you to come over here without any one to protect you."

"I am sorry you have come."

"That's complimentary, and I suppose my company is not agreeable."

"On the present occasion it is not."

"You are selfish, Phil. You wish to do a big thing all alone by yourself, and are afraid you will be robbed of a share of the glory."

"You know better, Larry."

"Then don't quarrel with me. You made such a row about coming over here under that old souppot, that I thought it was really a dangerous enterprise; but it is only child's play. Come, Phil, are you going to march on the Austrians?" he rattled on, so lightly that I was quite ashamed of my prudent measures. "Lead on; you shall boss the job, and I will follow you."

"All right; but you must do as I do, or you will not only imperil your own head, but mine."

"Right! You shall keep your head, and I will keep mine."

I crept out of the bushes, and throwing myself upon the ground, crawled to a ditch, used to irrigate the country. On one side of it was the usual row of mulberries, behind which we walked a short distance; but, as the water would not run up hill, we were forced to leave it in order to ascend the slope on which stood the tall tree. Several rows of mulberries extended up the declivity, and between the trees were lines of grape vines, whose luxuriant foliage afforded us a partial protection. Creeping on the ground, we soon reached the summit of the slope. Around us the ground was ploughed with shot and shell, and many of the trees were splintered; but the fire in this direction had been suspended, for the general knew where we were expected to be. The firing had driven back the pickets, and we could not yet even see them.

"Your plan has worked first rate, Phil," said my friend, as we paused on the rising ground to take an observation.

"All but the soup-kettle, which was superfluous," I replied, vexed at the coolness and indifference my companion had displayed.

"Not at all, my good fellow. If a single shot had hit your ark, of course I should not have dared to cross the river. The soup-kettle was a tip-top idea to feel your way with; but of course, after you had proved that there was not a picket within half a mile, it was not needed. It is scarcely necessary

CROSSING THE TICINO. Page 278.

for me to insinuate that I do not undervalue your ark of safety. No pickets in sight yet."

"No; but I must climb that tree. From the top of it I can see over the mulberries, and cover the country for miles."

On the summit of the slope the ground was planted with Indian corn, which was high enough to afford us all the shelter we needed. We crawled in the rows across several of the spaces between the lines of mulberries, till we reached the tree. There was not a branch on its trunk within seventy-five feet of the ground, and it was no easy job to climb it.

"There you are! Crawl up, my mud-turtle," said Larry, glancing at me.

Of course I could not swim the river without wetting my clothes, and as I crawled through the cornfield the soil had clung to my dripping garments till I well deserved the appellation which my companion had applied to me. But Larry was in no better condition.

"I am all ready, fellow-worm of the earth; but you must crawl over to the edge of the cornfield, so as to give me timely notice of the approach of the enemy, while I crawl up the tree."

"Right! we are a wormy couple. Crawl away."

My friend made his way to the point indicated, and I commenced my difficult undertaking. Fortunately, the tree was of the spindling kind, and its diameter did not at all correspond to its height. Even when my arms and legs were far shorter than now, I had climbed tall cotton-woods, and the experience I had acquired enabled me to accomplish my purpose. I was obliged frequently to pause and rest; but in less than half an hour I had ascended as far as it was safe to go. I had a full view of the country in every direction. The battle was still raging above us at Buffalora and other points. Vast volumes of smoke were rising from the battle-field, and the roar of artillery seemed to shake the earth beneath me. I turned to the country behind the slope. I distinctly saw several columns of infantry and artillery moving hurriedly towards Magenta. A large portion of them had been posted behind the earth-works, to repel an advance in this direction. I had ascertained what General Eberlé desired to know — that the troops behind the battery had been withdrawn. The Austrians were hard pressed by the Imperial Guard, and were obliged to reënforce their columns by bringing up the troops which had protected their left. I made the signal with my handkerchief, repeating it till I saw the pontoon train dash down to the river's side. The French artillery poured shot and shell into the earth-works with tremendous rapidity, in order to cover the operations of the pontoon engineers. In a very short time the bridge was completed. A regiment of Zouaves went over on the run, and, without stopping to fire a volley, or even a single shot, rushed upon the earth-works, carrying them in the twinkling of an eye. As the artillery-men retreated, their own guns were turned upon them. I saw the picket line which had been driven back from the river retire upon the main body. The field was clear, and our brigade released from its late inactivity. I descended from my high position, and found Larry at the foot of the tree.

"How's that for high?" said he.

"First rate. The Austrians have all left this vicinity, and our work is done. I want my coat and cap."

As we walked towards the pontoon bridge, we met the general.

"You have done ze business very nice. You

have help us very much. You have done one grand thing!" exclaimed he, grasping my hand.

"It was very easily done," I replied. "My friend swam over without any soup-kettle."

"Only after Phil had proved that there was no danger."

Our servant had brought over our clothes and baggage, and our horses were waiting near the bridge. We washed ourselves in the river, and put on clean shirts. Mounting our steeds, we overtook the brigade, and took our places near the general. The column was marching towards Magenta, where the heaviest of the fighting was now going on. Near a farm-house on the way we were confronted by a force of Austrians, and a sharp skirmish took place. I found myself in the midst of it, with bullets whistling about my head. The general gave me an order to deliver to a colonel, and I hastened to obey. I soon became interested in the business, and as zealous as any one on the field. In delivering another order, I found myself, by a sudden movement of the Austrians, directly in front of them; my horse dropped under me, and one of my struggles as a soldier was to get my leg out from beneath him.

All the rest of that day was a hot struggle. We

drove the Austrians before us at last, and entered the village of Magenta. We took the place house by house, and street by street. All was fury and excitement; but it was victory — hard-won victory. Larry was as wild as any Frenchman on the field, and, when sent to execute an order, finding the officer in command of the battalion killed, he led the column himself, and made a fierce charge with it. Both of us were repeatedly commended by our friend the general.

The day at Magenta was won, and that night I saw the emperor and the king of Italy. I was utterly exhausted when the work was done, and while the entire plain was ringing with cheers, I went to sleep.

The next day, and the next, we marched. The allied army entered Milan. The two sovereigns were received with acclamations. Our brigade was encamped on the outskirts of the city. As soon as we could obtain leave, we hastened to the *Corso di Bosinare*. I found the office of Signor Bertani, and ascertained where his residence was. Taking a carriage, we hastened thither. It was quite near our camp.

I was admitted, and in a few minutes I stood in the presence of my mother.

CHAPTER XXI.

IN WHICH PHIL IS IDENTIFIED BY HIS MOTHER, AND LARRY GOES TO ENGLAND.

I STOOD before my mother. I trembled with emotion. For years I had been looking forward to this moment with bounding anticipations. It had seemed to me that all the joys of earthly life were concentrated in this instant. Like a little child, I had longed and sighed for my mother. I could not speak; I could only look at her. I could see in her face, which was more beautiful to me than that of the fairest maiden I had ever beheld, the expression and every feature of the picture in my possession.

But I could not forget that my identity had not yet been acknowledged. In the room were Mr. Joseph Collingsby and his invalid wife. Perhaps I should be spurned here, as I had been in Chicago, when I attempted to claim my birthright. The events of the past rushed through my mind with electric rapidity, and I tried to connect the past with the present. I gazed at the lady before me with tremulous anxiety. I saw that she was regarding me with equal earnestness. I tried to speak, but I could not, and we stood gazing at each other in silence.

At the door I had simply inquired for Mr. Collingsby; but as the Italian servant did not speak French, I could do nothing more than mention the name. It appeared that the party were expecting the arrival of two English gentlemen, with whom they desired to make the journey into Switzerland; and we were taken to be those persons, and admitted without ceremony.

"You wish to see me?" said Mr. Collingsby to Larry Grimsby.

"No, sir; my friend desires to see Mrs. Farringford."

"What is your friend's name?"

"Philip Farringford."

I heard this, and my mother heard it, while we were still regarding each other. Suddenly the lady threw herself upon my neck, and kissed me on the cheek. I felt her hot tears upon my face, and I felt that I was recognized without any exhibition of the evidence. I kissed her in return.

"Louise!" said Mr. Collingsby, sternly.

She gently disengaged herself from me, and taking one of my hands in hers, she looked at her brother.

"Well, Joseph?" she replied, struggling with her emotions.

"I must beg you to be cautious."

"This is my son!" exclaimed she, grasping my other hand also, and gazing at me again with the most intense earnestness.

"Father and Richard have both warned you against this person," said Mr. Collingsby, coldly.

I must explain what afterwards came to my knowledge. My mother had been told that her husband had acknowledged a young man as his son; but her father's family in Chicago believed that it was a trick to obtain a portion of the old man's property. She had been informed that I was on the way to Europe, and cautioned to repel the imposition if I came into her presence. It was only by accident that I was admitted to her presence — an accident made possible only by the alarms of war. The party had been trying for

Phil finds his Mother. Page 288.

several weeks to get into Switzerland; but Mr. Collingsby was a timid man, and dared not undertake the journey in the troubled state of the country. They were in daily expectation of the arrival of the two English gentlemen who were to accompany them, and doubtless Mr. Collingsby was very much disappointed when the visitors proved to be other persons.

"Joseph, I know him," said my mother; and she smiled through her tears.

"This is absurd, Louise. Your child was lost when he was only two years old."

"But I know his expression, and I know every lineament of his face. It is my boy — I know it!"

"It is ridiculous, Louise."

"I ask for no evidence whatever but his face. It is exactly the same as when he last looked upon me," added my mother, still gazing earnestly at me.

"I will not permit this imposition," protested Mr. Collingsby.

"I know my own child, and I shall cling to him while I have life."

"Right! That's the style," whispered Larry.

"Mr. Collingsby, neither your father nor your brother would ever listen to what my father or I had to say on this subject. I offered to present the evidence to them, but they declined to hear me."

"It was too absurd to be listened to."

"Reasonable people do not judge until after they have heard," I replied.

"But the whole story is ridiculous on the face of it."

"Sit down, Philip, and tell *me* all about it," said my mother, leading me to a sofa.

"Not here," interposed Mr. Collingsby.

"Then I will go with you, Philip, to your hotel."

"Are you crazy, Louise?" demanded her brother.

"Will you hear what my son has to say?"

"No, I will not. It is all a trick of his drunken father," said Mr. Collingsby, angrily.

"My father is a sober, industrious, Christian man. He does not ask a dollar or a penny of any Collingsby. He is able to support his family, and asks no favors of any one. I know that he has not drank a drop of intoxicating liquor for two years," I replied, warmly.

"Joseph, this is my son. If you repel him, you repel me. Where he goes I will go. I have nothing more to say," added my mother, with quiet dignity, as she threw her arm around my neck.

"I am sorry that the warnings of father and Richard have had no effect upon you," said he, more calmly, when he saw that his violence was complicating the matter.

"Until I saw Philip I believed that it was an imposition; now I know that it is not. This is my son. I cannot be mistaken," replied my mother.

"I think, sir, that if you will hear me, I can convince you."

"Not now; another time," he answered, testily.

"I am not quite prepared at the present time myself to exhibit all the evidence," I added. "If you will name a time, you will oblige me."

"To morrow, at ten o'clock," said Mr. Collingsby.

"I have sent to Genoa for my trunk, and expect it to-day. If it comes I shall be able to satisfy you, I think."

"But you must not leave me for a moment, Philip," said my mother.

"I am a volunteer aid in the French army, on the staff of General Eberlé, mother."

"You?"

"I was in the battle of Magenta."

"O, Philip! — how could you — "

"But I will resign at once."

"Then I must," added Larry. "But I will go over to the camp. If your trunk has come, shall I send it over here?"

"Certainly not," I replied.

"Yes, send it," interposed my mother. "And your own also, if you are the friend of my son."

"But, Louise," interposed Mr. Collingsby.

"If my son is not welcome here, I cannot be. I will go to a hotel with him then. He shall not leave me," said my mother.

"I cannot trespass upon the hospitality of strangers," I interposed. "I must go to the camp, mother, in order to resign my position."

"If you leave me, I am afraid I shall never see you again. I will go with you to the camp," added my mother.

Mr. Collingsby protested. He was evidently disgusted, and only wished to get me out of the way. Signora Bertani appeared, and invited both

Larry and me to make her house our home. We did not accept, though we staid there till after dinner. Then we went to the camp, resigned our positions on the staff, and bade farewell to our comrades in arms, who were very kind to us. The general expressed his regret at parting with us, and offered to serve us in any way he could. He gave each of us a testimonial, and obtained for us a safe-conduct at headquarters, which would enable us to pass any army lines, and which would procure any assistance that we might require. My trunk had arrived, and we went to the Hotel Marino.

We returned to the residence of Signor Bertani. My mother embraced me as I entered, and said that the hour I had been absent was an age to her. I exhibited my testimonial and our safe-conduct, and translated them into English, for Mr. Collingsby knew hardly a word of French. The document attracted his attention, for we could pass his party through into Switzerland. He was more considerate towards me then, for he was very anxious to escape from Italy and the confusion of the war. I staid till a late hour, and then went to the hotel.

The next morning, with the relics of my childhood, I hastened to the Bertanis. Mr. Collingsby was not inclined to hear me, but he could not avoid it without driving my mother and me from the house.

"Now, Philip, I want you to tell the whole story," said my mother, who was seated at my side, holding my hand.

"I am afraid it will take me two or three hours," I replied.

"No matter if it takes all day."

I related my story from beginning to end, and it was lunch time when I finished.

"That is a very good story; but there is nothing at all in it to convince anybody that you are my sister's son," said Mr. Collingsby, after we returned from the dining-room.

"I am aware of it — the evidence is yet to be presented. When I was discovered by Matt Rockwood, certain articles were found upon me."

"You were wrapped in a shawl. How well I remember it!" said my mother.

"Here is the shawl," I added, taking it from the bundle at my side.

"It is the same one!" exclaimed my mother.

I produced the little dress, and the bracelets with which the sleeves had been looped up, which were promptly identified.

"This locket was hung upon my neck," I continued.

"You gave this locket to the child yourself, Joseph," said my mother, opening it. "Here is the picture painted by Schmidt."

Mr. Collingsby examined it, and admitted that the locket was the one he had given me.

"But where did you get these things, young man?"

"They were found upon me when I was picked up by Matt Rockwood."

He suggested the same objections that others had presented. The relics were good evidence as far as they went, but they did not identify me.

"But I identify him," interposed my mother. "Could I look into his little face every day, all day long, for two years, and not know him again? After I lost him, I still saw him, and his image has never passed out of my heart. I can see him now as he was then."

"Was there any mark upon him, Louise, such as is discovered upon the foundlings and the long-lost sons in the novels?" laughed Mr. Collingsby.

"Not a mark," I replied.

"Yes, he had a mole on the back of his neck; but that may be gone now," added my mother, drawing down my head, and examining the part indicated. "But I should not be any better satisfied if I found a dozen marks which I had seen upon the child. There it is — larger than it was, but in the same place."

"I give it up," said Mr. Collingsby, when he had examined the mole. "Give me your hand, Philip. You are my nephew, without doubt. But it is a strange story, and you must excuse my incredulity."

"I don't blame you at all, uncle Joseph."

"Now, can you get us out of Italy?" asked my uncle; and perhaps his desire to escape from war's alarms had no little influence in convincing him that I was his nephew.

"Certainly I can. You shall start to-day, if you please."

"To-morrow will do."

We made the arrangements for the journey at once.

"Now tell me about your father," said my mother. "Is he entirely changed?"

"Entirely, mother; and I am sure that he will never drink another drop as long as he lives."

"Thank God!"

"I hope you will forgive him, mother."

"With all my heart, if he is changed. We may be happy yet; but O, what a waste of misery there is behind me!"

"Never mind the past, mother; let us think only of the future."

"You are right, Philip. I can hardly believe that I am the mother of such a manly boy as you are — so brave and daring, too. But I do believe it, and this fact is happiness enough for the future. I should be content to live in a hovel now."

"There will be no need of that, for father has a salary of three thousand dollars, and I am good for a thousand more," I added.

"But I am afraid we cannot go home at present, for Joseph's wife is very feeble, and I cannot leave her. I wish your father could come over and join us."

"That is impossible, for he has the care of Mr. Rockwood's property in St. Louis, and cannot leave. I shall write to him to-day, and send the good news."

At a late hour in the evening I went to the hotel, and wrote a long letter to my father. The next day we went by easy stages in a private carriage to Sesto, at the foot of Lake Maggiore. Our safe-conduct enabled us to pass without difficulty, and procured for us the best accommodations on the road. The health of Mrs. Collingsby was so feeble that we used up a week in travelling to Lucerne. By this time I was on excellent terms with my uncle. I took charge of the details of the journey, which my knowledge of French enabled me to do better than he could. Larry and I had written to our banker in Paris to forward our letters to Lucerne. There was one for my friend, and several for me.

"I must go at once, Phil," said Larry, after he had opened his letter.

"Why? what's the matter?"

"'Come home at once, you dog, or you will never again see me alive,'" replied Larry, reading from his letter. "And it was written a week ago. I must not lose a moment."

"But I don't see how I can go with you, Larry."

"I must go alone, then. My grandfather may

be dead now. He is a jolly old fellow, and I hope he won't slip off this time."

"I hope not. You must look out for Miles Grimsby: he means harm to you."

"Confound him! I don't care what he means. There will be a coldness between us now, since I have discovered his game — that is all:"

"Cuore is still in the hospital, and the last I heard of him he was getting better; but be prudent, Larry, and don't make any friends on the way. I wish I were going with you."

"I wish you were, my boy; but you must write every day, and I will do the same, if it is only a single line."

"I will, Larry; and I shall miss you very much."

"But you have your mother now."

"Thank God, I have."

He was off that night, after bidding us an affectionate adieu. We missed him very much, for he was always full of life and fun.

CHAPTER XXII.

IN WHICH PHIL REMONSTRATES WITH LARRY, WHO DECIDES TO GO UP IN A BALLOON.

REMOVED from the din and excitement of war, Mrs. Collingsby's health improved. We went to Carlsbad, whose waters had a very salutary effect upon her; and she was so much better that my mother and I made several journeys to places of interest in the interior of Europe, as Berlin, Dresden, Vienna, Frankfort, Cologne, Hamburg, and Baden-Baden. The war ended with the battle of Solferino and the treaty of Villa-Franca.

I had frequent letters from Larry. Sir Philip Grimsby was not dead when his grandson arrived, though he was very feeble. Miles was utterly confounded at the return of my friend, who became a great favorite with the baronet. In October, while we were still at Carlsbad, Larry wrote me that Sir Philip was nearly restored in health, and consented to his absence for a few weeks. I had scarcely received the letter before my friend arrived. We almost hugged each other in the mutual delight of meeting again. He was cordially welcomed by my mother and my uncle.

"Tell me about Grimsby Hall, Larry. How is your grandfather?" I said, when we were by ourselves.

"He is better; but I think he is failing, on the whole. His constitution seems to be broken, and another stroke of apoplexy will finish him. But he is a jolly old fellow."

"And how is Miles?"

"I didn't see much of him. Miles has taken to yachting, and is spending piles of money on his boat."

"I didn't think he had wit enough to appreciate a yacht."

"I don't know about that; but he is completely absorbed in his craft, and says he shall go to America in her next season."

"How big is his yacht?"

"About a hundred tons, I saw by a report of a sailing match, in which she took the second prize."

"I wouldn't be Miles Grimsby for all the yachts that ever floated; but I envy him the pleasure of such an amusement. There is nothing like it, to my mind. I should like to make a trip around Europe, stopping a week or so in places of interest on the way. But I shall never have the means to do anything of that kind."

"I shall, Phil, for my grandfather allows me just the same as Miles has — ten thousand pounds a year; and when either of us wishes to buy a yacht, a pair of horses, or a house, he is willing to come down with an extra ten thousand or so. I rather like the idea of a voyage in a yacht, and we will talk it over."

"Of course I don't expect you to buy a yacht for my benefit."

"I shall enjoy it as much as you, Phil."

"You say that Blanche is well and happy."

"I said she was well — not happy. I don't think she is happy. I didn't tell you that we are engaged, but it is so."

"Indeed!"

"Fact; and we were engaged before the baronet acknowledged me as his grandson."

"Then you are publicly acknowledged."

"Not very publicly — only to a dozen or so; and it hadn't got into the newspapers when I left England, so far as I know."

"If you and Blanche are engaged, I should think she would be happy," I suggested.

"So far as our engagement is concerned, I think she is happy. But Grimsby Hall is not a pleasant place for her to live. Uncle Miles is only one step from lunacy, and he makes the house very uncomfortable. They say his brain is softening; but I don't believe he ever had any brains to soften. Once in a while he has a tantrum, and makes the house too hot for the family. I had to take him by the collar one night, when he insisted upon turning his wife out of doors. But he is simply stupid most of the time, and they think of sending him to an asylum. But what are you going to do, Phil?"

"I hardly know."

"Shall you go home this fall?"

"If Mrs. Collingsby's health will permit, we shall."

"By the way, I think I saw Cuore in London," continued Larry.

"Impossible."

"Not at all impossible. The last we heard of him in the hospital, he was better."

"Where did you see him?"

"In the railroad station, as I was leaving for Paris. He seemed to have an eye on me, but when I made for him, he disappeared. In Paris I kept both eyes open, for I fancied that the rascal was dogging my steps. Miles was up at the Hall the Sunday before I left, and knew where I was going. Several times, when the train stopped between here and Paris, I looked into every compartment of the carriages, and examined the face of every passenger; but I did not see Cuore."

"Did you say anything to Miles about him?" I asked.

"Not a word; nor to Sir Philip. I don't think the old man likes Miles, though he treats him with a show of affection, and all that sort of thing."

"But you don't think Miles will attempt to repeat the experiment he tried before?"

"I don't know why he should not, for I still stand between him and his expectations. But he was very pleasant to me, and invited me to sail with him in his yacht. I was afraid I might fall overboard if I did; so I declined," laughed Larry. "I shall keep my eyes open. I hope you are not going to stay here long, Phil. It's a stupid place."

I should have thought so myself if my mother had not been with me. We were never tired of being together, and of talking of the past. Mrs. Collingsby was so much better that it was decided to return to America. We went to Leipsic, and found the city crowded with people, in attendance upon a great festival. With difficulty we obtained rooms at the Hotel de Pologne. In the evening Larry and I went to the great garden, which was crowded with visitors, drinking beer and listening to the music. We seated ourselves at a table, and drank coffee.

"There he is!" exclaimed Larry, pointing towards the kiosk in which the musicians played.

"Who?"

"Cuore."

Larry leaped to his feet, and moved in the direction he had pointed; but the surging crowd came between us and the man we were seeking.

"He is gone," said Larry. "He sat at this table. There is his beer, not finished."

"Are you sure it was he? I did not see him."

"I am pretty sure it was he, though he was not dressed as when we saw him before."

"Perhaps you are mistaken."

"I may be, but I don't think I am. If it was not he, why should he dodge so suddenly when I moved this way?"

"Possibly you are right."

"I know the rascal's face too well to be mistaken. The moment he caught my eye, he turned away."

We returned to our table and drank the coffee which was waiting for us. We walked all over the garden in search of Cuore, but were unable to find him. I came to the conclusion that my friend had been mistaken in the identity of the person he supposed to be his enemy.

"Can you read that, Phil?" asked Larry, as he paused before a handbill on which was the picture of a balloon.

"Not a word of it," I replied. "But evidently there is to be a balloon ascension here."

"Did you ever go up in a balloon, Phil?"

"Of course I never did."

"Of course you would like to do so."

"No; I don't believe in exposing myself to danger in that way."

"'Pon my word, there is no danger in it," laughed Larry. "Did you ever hear of a man being killed in a balloon?"

"I have heard of people being killed by falling out of them."

"Did you ever hear of a person being killed by falling out of a carriage?"

"Certainly I have."

"Then it is dangerous to ride in a carriage."

"That is sophistry, not argument, Larry."

"I am no philosopher, as you are, learned Phil. I don't know that I ever heard of anybody being killed by an accident to a balloon, except a woman in France, when the thing was blown up by a sky-rocket, or something of that sort. If I could get a chance to go up, even by paying a hundred dollars or so, I should go up. It would be a new sensation."

We went back to the hotel. In the office was the balloon handbill. Larry stopped to look at it again.

"Donnerstag. What's that, Phil?" said he, spelling out a word on the bill.

"I haven't the least idea; but I judge from the date following it, that it is some day of the week."

"Exactly so. Donnerstag. If I wasn't a printer, I couldn't read even that."

"It means Thursday," said a dark-complexioned gentleman, who had apparently paused to read the bill.

"Thank you. That's to-morrow."

"Yes. You do not read German."

"Not a word of it."

"The balloon ascension is to take place to-morrow, at four o'clock in the afternoon," continued the stranger.

"Fifty thalers!" exclaimed Larry, reading from the bill. "That is a pretty steep price for seeing a balloon ascension."

"Steep?" queried the stranger.

"Very dear," explained Larry.

"Not for seeing it. Signor Bianchi, the aeronaut, will take two gentlemen with him, as passengers, for fifty thalers each."

"Cheap enough. I should like to see Signor Bianchi."

"Should you?"

"Are his passengers engaged yet?"

"No."

"Then I should like to see him. Does he speak English?"

"Perfectly," replied the stranger, smiling. "As well as I do."

"That's well enough."

"Will you see him?"

"Certainly."

"You don't really think of going up in a balloon, Larry," I interposed.

"'Pon my word, I do, if I get the chance; and I am willing to pay fifty thalers, cash down, for the opportunity."

"Signor Bianchi is staying at this hotel," said the stranger.

"I beg your pardon; but are you an Italian?" asked Larry.

"I am."

"Perhaps you are Signor Bianchi."

"No; but I travel all over Europe with him, and sometimes make an ascension. If you desire to go up in the balloon to-morrow, you shall have a place."

"I will give you a final answer in half an hour or so."

The gentleman bowed, and left us.

"Don't think of such a thing, Larry," I entreated, when we were alone. "Don't risk your neck for nothing."

"Not for nothing. I am to pay fifty thalers for the privilege of risking it, and I think it is cheap at that."

"But it is folly."

"Certainly it is. But I am human. Phil, I must go up in that balloon; I can't help it. I always had a desire to do the thing. You remember there was one in Marseilles when we were there. I was telling Cuore then — who said he had been up five times — if I ever got a chance, I should certainly go up."

"Don't you do it, Larry. This man is an Italian, too."

"No matter if he is. He is one of those balloonists that travel over the country, and make ascensions at fairs and festivals, and for the benefit of beer gardens, and such places. I am afraid if I lose this opportunity I shall never get another."

In vain I begged and pleaded with him; he was as obstinate as a mule. Mr. Collingsby and my mother tried their eloquence upon him with no better result.

"I have concluded to go," said Larry, walking up to the Italian, who was seated in the coffee-room..

"Very well, sir. I will give you a receipt for fifty thalers."

"Are you the proprietor of the balloon?"

"I am; but I am not the gentleman who makes the ascension to-morrow."

"You are not Signor Bianchi?"

"No. I am Signor Cuore, his partner."

"Cuore!" exclaimed Larry.

"Cuore, sir."

He certainly was not the villain of that name whom we knew.

"Have you a brother?"

"One in New York; none here," replied the balloonist. "I have lived five years in New York myself."

"Where is Signor Bianchi?"

"He has retired for the night."

". I should rather like to see the man with whom I am to go up."

"He has been quite sick for a week; but he is better. He may not be able to make the ascension to-morrow. If not, I shall go up in his place.

If you wish to engage a seat in the car, I will give you a receipt now, for we have other applications."

"I engage it here and now;" and Larry took the fifty thalers from his pocket-book.

"If you will give me your card, I will write the receipt," added Cuore.

Larry wrote his name on a card, and the balloonist made out the receipt in good English.

"Are there any other Italians in Leipsic?" I asked, when the business was finished.

"Plenty of them," replied Cuore.

"Do you know another of your name?"

"Yes; two of them. Cuore is a very common name in Italy. One of them is a wine merchant, and the other is a silk agent from Milan."

I described the Cuore in my own mind; but the Italian did not know him, or professed not to know him. Larry was confident that he had seen our evil genius in the garden. There was nothing improbable in the supposition that the villain was in Leipsic, and that he was following us wherever we went. He was certainly in the employ of Miles Grimsby. He had failed in his wicked purpose once, but he might not a second or a third time. I could not connect him in any manner with the balloon; but, then, his ways were dark.

"Larry, I beg of you, as a favor, not to go up in the balloon to-morrow," said I, as we went to our room.

"Nonsense, Phil!"

"Cuore is in town, according to your statement; and this balloon man is also a Cuore. There is something wrong somewhere."

"Don't be a baby, Phil."

"I begin to see through the whole of it. Cuore has been dogging you since you left London. He knows — for you told him — that you intended to go up in a balloon when you got a chance; so he has laid in with this man to take you up; and he will take care that you do not come down alive."

"If I don't, he won't," laughed Larry. "Don't make bugbears, my dear Phil. Your brain is disordered. Go to sleep, and you will wake up better in the morning. Adieu."

Larry was still obstinate, and I went to sleep.

CHAPTER XXIII.

IN WHICH PHIL IS VERY ANXIOUS ABOUT LARRY, WHO HAS A PERILOUS ADVENTURE IN THE BALLOON.

IN the morning letters for our party came, forwarded by the banker. One had an ominous black seal, and was addressed to Larry. I handed it to him.

"You will not go up in the balloon to-day," I said; for I concluded that the letter announced the death of Sir Philip Grimsby.

"Perhaps not," he replied; and I saw that he was deeply moved. "If my grandfather is dead, I shall never cease to blame myself for leaving him, even for a single day."

He opened the letter. The event of its coming seemed to be something like a providence interposing to prevent him from risking his life so foolhardily in the balloon.

"Thank God it is not my grandfather!" exclaimed Larry; and I could see the feeling of relief that found expression in his face.

"But who is it?"

"My uncle Miles. I have rather expected it. Well, it is a mercy to him, and certainly to the other members of the family, for he was of no use or comfort to himself or anybody else. But this letter is a week old, and the day of the funeral has already gone by."

"Yet you will not go up in a balloon after receiving such a letter," I suggested.

"Why not? It is not a ball or a party."

"But it is a frolic."

"Not at all. I go up in the balloon for the same reason that I should visit a picture gallery or a library — to improve my mind, to obtain larger views of things in general."

My friend was determined to carry out his purpose, and it was useless for me to labor any further to dissuade him. At the appointed time we went to the garden, where the balloon was already inflated. There were thousands of spectators, most of whom had probably never seen an ascension. The Cuore whom we had met at the hotel requested Larry to take his seat in the car.

"Good by, Larry," said I, shaking his hand.

"Nonsense, Phil! I shall be with you this evening or to-morrow morning," replied he, lightly. "The only danger that I ever could see in going up in a balloon was being carried out to sea; but that is impossible here, you know. I am perfectly safe, in my own opinion."

"Of course I shall hope for the best. Have you seen the man who is going up with you?"

"Not yet."

"I expect him in a moment," interposed Cuore. "As I told you, he is not very well, and I told him not to come till four o'clock."

The crowd cheered and applauded when Larry seated himself in the car. Twenty men held the balloon by the netting, and it was permitted slowly to rise till the car was lifted from the ground.

"Where is the other passenger?" asked Larry.

"You will be the only one," replied Cuore. "The gas is so poor, I find, that we cannot take the second gentleman."

"All right. Then I shall have the fun all to myself," added Larry.

"Here is Bianchi."

I turned to see the aeronaut. He was enveloped in a long overcoat, which extended down to his ankles. It had a cowl, which was drawn over his cap, so that he looked like a monk. He walked directly to the car and leaped in. At the same instant Cuore on the ground cut the single rope that held the balloon. A wild cheer from the crowd rent the air as it rose almost perpendicularly. Bianchi waved a couple of flags, and the multitude shouted again. I obtained a single glance at the cowled head of the aeronaut after he started. He seemed like a mysterious personage to me, so sudden and so singular had been his coming, and so rapid his going. Larry was seated in the bottom of the car, and I did not see his face after the ascent commenced. In spite of all I had said, I could not but feel that the chances were altogether in favor of my friend's coming back alive and well.

I watched the balloon till it looked like a speck in the distance. It floated off to the westward, towards the Harz Mountains. In spite of myself I was nervous and uneasy about my friend. I could not adopt his theory that he was just as safe up in a balloon, a mile or two from the earth, as he was on the solid ground. The time hung heavily upon me till night, and then I could not sleep for thinking of Larry. I was sorry I had not been more decided with him; that I had not induced my party to leave Leipsic before the ascension.

The morning papers contained no intelligence of the aeronauts. I was told by the porter, to whom I applied for information, that Cuore, the balloonist's partner, had departed for Cassel, where he was to make arrangements for another ascension at a fair, and where Bianchi was to convey the balloon after its descent. Our party were ready to continue the journey to England, and were only waiting the return of Larry. At dark he had not arrived, and I became very anxious about him. But the porter came to me with an evening paper, in which was a paragraph saying that the balloon had descended near Nordhausen, at the extremity of the Harz Mountains.

"When will he return?" I asked.

"Not to-night. It is more as sixty miles, mit a railroad only from Halle," replied the porter.

"Here he is!" I actually shouted, as Larry entered the office, covered with mud from head to foot.

"*Jawohl!*" exclaimed the porter.

"How are you, Phil?" said my friend, grasping my offered hand.

"First rate; only I have worried my life out about you," I replied. "What's the matter?"

He looked pale, and seemed to be exhausted. I was sure he was not satisfied with his journey in the air.

"I'm tired, Phil; that's all. I want some supper."

We went to our room, after ordering his supper, where he changed his clothes. But he was weary and languid, for him.

"Where did you land, Larry?"

"I haven't the least idea. Don't know the name of a single town through which I passed," said he, with a faint smile. "I couldn't speak a word of the lingo, and no one spoke English."

"But where was Bianchi?"

"Bianchi?"

"The balloonist."

"Humph! He wasn't there. But let me have some supper before I say anything. Don't ask me another question, Phil."

I saw that something unpleasant had occurred; but I waited until after he had taken his supper, when he declared that he felt better.

"Now, Phil, we will go up stairs, and I will tell you all about it," said he.

In the chamber he threw himself upon a lounge.

"Did you see the man who went up with me, Phil?"

"I did."

"Did you know him?"

"No. He did not show himself till the moment you started, and I could not see his face, which was nearly covered by the cowl of his coat."

"Who do you think he was?"

"Bianchi, I supposed."

"Not at all."

"Who was he?"

"Cuore."

"You don't mean so."

"The fellow we talked with here was Bianchi; and he is the man who usually makes the ascensions."

"But you don't mean to say that your companion in the balloon was the Cuore we knew in Italy."

"I do. I was sure I saw him in the garden, though you did not believe me. He was the very man. I did not see his face till we were half a mile above the earth. He stood with his back towards me, waving the flags. I did not feel quite at home in the basket, though, as I sat in the bottom of the car, I was not conscious of any motion. Then I looked over the side, and the view was so magnificent that I could not help shouting with rapture. It was the sublimest thing in the world. Phil, I advise you to go up in a balloon when you get a chance; but don't go up with such a fellow as Cuore."

"I certainly shall not, if I can help it. How long was it before you recognized your companion?"

"When he had waved the flags a while, he threw back his cowl and turned round. I knew him at once, though he was very much altered in appearance. He was dressed better, and wore a longer beard. He looked at me, and, if ever a man was ugly, he was.

"'Cuore!' said I.

"'At your service,' he replied.

"I told him that I supposed we did not meet by accident; but he made no reply, and did not seem to be ready for business. We floated over towns and villages, and were approaching the hills to the westward at sunset. The balloon began to drop, and Cuore threw out bags of sand till we rose again. I suggested that it was nearly dark, and that we had better make a landing.

"'I purpose to stay up all night,' said he.

"'All right,' I replied.

"But, having used up all his ballast, the balloon dropped down into a lower atmosphere, and began to go to the eastward, in another current.

"'This will never do,' said Cuore. 'I want to go over the Harz Mountains, for we make an ascension in Cassel. The balloon will rise no higher with both of us in the car.'

"'And you would like to throw me out,' I suggested.

"'No,' he replied, 'I would not do such a thing.'

"I told him plainly that he was in the employ of Miles Grimsby; that he had dogged me from London, and that the present excursion was for my benefit. The balloon was now slowly nearing the earth, and to help it along, I gave the valve rope a pull, for I was in a hurry to have my dangerous companion where I could be on equal terms with him. The moment I touched it, he clinched me by the throat, and attempted to throw me out of the car. I was desperate then, as any man would be in such a situation. He was not so strong as he supposed he was, for he had not entirely recovered from his wounds. In the midst of the struggle, I

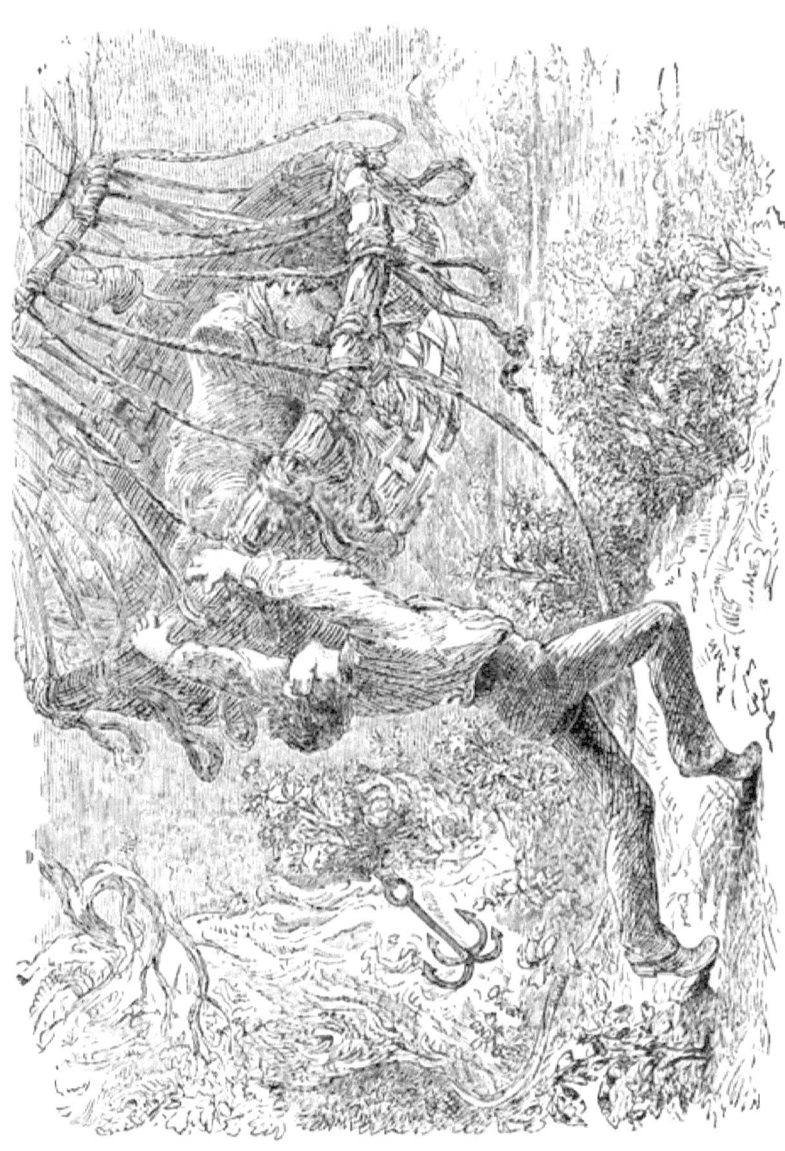

LARRY'S ESCAPE FROM THE BALLOON. Page 323.

heard him groan heavily. I don't know, but I think that, in his violent exertions, he opened the old wound, for he fell back upon the ropes by which the basket was suspended. I pulled him down into the bottom of the car. He would have fallen out if I had not done so, and I did not wish to serve him as he intended to serve me. I would not have his death upon my conscience for all the revenues of Grimsby. He was not insensible, but he seemed to be in great pain.

"In the struggle my legs had become entangled in the valve rope, and the pressure upon it kept it open. The balloon descended steadily, and soon touched the ground upon the side of a hill. There was not a breath of air, and the instant the car reached ground I threw over the grapnel, and leaped out, intending to hold on to the basket. I knew nothing about ballooning, and I was too much excited to think. I supposed the grapnel would hold the thing; but the moment the balloon was relieved of my weight it shot up into the air again. I lost my hold upon the basket, for it went up with a jerk the instant my feet touched the earth. The grapnel rope was wound around the trunk of a tree, and ran out of the car, to which it did not appear to be fastened. Relieved of my weight, and of that of the grapnel and rope, the balloon rose, moving first to the eastward, and then, as its altitude increased, to the westward.

"Now, Phil, I didn't mean to leave Cuore in that car. I hope I had enough of your Christian spirit about me to do what I could for him in his disabled condition, though he sought my life, and will again, if he recovers."

"But what did you do, Larry?"

"I could not do anything for Cuore, and not much for myself. A dozen men, women, and children gathered around me, and looked at me with wonder and astonishment. Probably they had been watching the balloon, and hastened to the spot when they saw it descending. One of them spoke to me, but of course I couldn't understand him. I spoke English to the group, but no one comprehended it. I showed some money, and said, 'Leipsic,' a dozen times. I made all sorts of signs, and was finally conducted to a house. I continued to repeat 'Leipsic' until the people comprehended what I wanted, and conveyed me in a cart to the nearest town. At the little hotel a man was brought to me who spoke a little

English. I told him I had come in the balloon, and wished to go back to Leipsic as soon as possible. I was told that a diligence would pass through the place in the middle of the night. I had some supper, and then tried to sleep; but I could not. My nerves were more shaken than ever before. At midnight I took the diligence, and came to a place where I took the train; and here I am, nearer used up than I ever was before."

"That's a very strange adventure," I added.

"Strange! I am beginning to lose my taste for adventure. I can't help thinking how I felt when Cuore attempted to pitch me out of the balloon. The idea of dropping down half a mile, and fetching up with a round turn on a rock, or even on the ground, was the most disagreeable thing that ever came over me. MORAL. When you go up in a balloon, get introduced to your companion before you start."

"What do you suppose has become of Cuore?"

"I haven't the least idea; but I suppose the balloon has come down before this time. I must go to bed, Phil, for I am used up."

I found my mother in the private parlor, and

repeated the adventure of my friend to an interested little audience.

Larry was better the next day, and we proceeded on our journey.

"I don't understand how Cuore came in that balloon," said I, as we rode along in the railway carriage.

"It is plain enough to me now, for I thought it all over while I was riding in that diligence. Cuore dogged me all the time, watching his chance to do something. He must have heard me say I wanted to go up in a balloon. Then he made a trade with Bianchi to go in his place."

"But why did Bianchi call himself Cuore?"

"Probably to blind me, and to provoke an inquiry in regard to the real Cuore, so that he could convince us there was no such Italian in Leipsic."

"Very likely. I hope you won't go up in a balloon again."

"I don't know. I think it pays, if you know your companion."

We continued on our journey, but did not reach London until the end of a week.

CHAPTER XXIV.

IN WHICH PHIL AND LARRY VISIT GRIMSBY HALL, AND
RETURN TO AMERICA.

LARRY had written to Sir Philip that our party would be in London at a certain time, and on our arrival he found a letter from the baronet, inviting us all to Grimsby Hall. We went after a day in the great city. Larry and I had letters from the president of the Lowerville Bank, acknowledging full satisfaction for all that was due the bank. My friend's letter, being the last one, assured him that the "honorable conduct" of the friends of Mr. Fennimore had placed his reputation above reproach. Though I was unable to see how this could be, I was willing to accept the fact. The directors were men of the world, it appeared afterwards, and losing no money by the cashier, they were willing and glad to acquit him of all evil intentions. They circulated the story that he was partially insane, and never meant to rob the bank of a dollar. His subsequent death, and the prompt settlement of all his accounts with the bank, appeared to confirm the statement, and his conduct was all "explained away."

All this was decidedly wrong, for the explanations were all pure inventions; but so far as Mr. Fennimore was concerned, he bitterly repented of his crime, and made all the restitution to the bank in his power. He deserved to be forgiven, but not to be "whitewashed."

We went to Grimsby Hall. The family were in deep mourning for Miles, senior, so far as outward appearances were concerned, but there was no genuine grief. Miles the younger was at home, but he was silent, moody, and cross-grained. We were cordially welcomed by the baronet and Blanche, but by no one else; and our party were not disposed to remain long.

"Miles, my boy, don't be so stiff with your cousin," said Sir Philip, as we sat in the library, on the evening of our arrival, after my mother and the Collingsbys had retired.

"I'm not stiff, sir," replied he.

"'Pon my life you are. I think you hate him."

"Certainly not, sir," protested Miles.

"It isn't his fault that he is your cousin, and the son of your father's older brother."

"I know it, sir, and I don't blame him. I have tried to treat him well, though I was a little irritated when I first saw that he came between me and my expectations."

"I don't want to have any muss about it," interposed Larry; "but I don't think he has tried very hard to treat me well."

"For what took place in the railway carriage when we were going to London, I beg your pardon," replied Miles, trying to look penitent.

"Apology cheerfully accepted," added Larry.

"What was that?" asked the baronet. "You never said anything to me about it."

"No, I did not, grandfather, for I don't want to be the author of a family row."

"I am very much obliged to him for his forbearance," replied Miles. "I think he has no further cause of complaint."

"Unfortunately, I have," said Larry; and I saw that he was determined to expose the conduct of Miles.

"What have you been doing, Miles?" demanded the baronet, sternly.

"Nothing at all, grandfather. Except in the instance for which I have apologized, I have never spoken an unkind word to him."

"That is very true, Miles; but you have done worse than that. You have employed an Italian bravo to dog my steps, and take my life, and twice I have narrowly escaped death at his hands."

"'Pon my life!" exclaimed the baronet, springing to his feet, his face red with anger.

"I really do not know what he means, Sir Philip," replied Miles, with an assumed look of amazement.

"I was here three months in the summer, and did not mention the circumstance," continued Larry; "but I confess I don't like to have a cutthroat on my track always. It isn't pleasant to be obliged to be on the lookout for an assassin all the time."

"I should say not," added the baronet, decidedly. "Are you so bad as this, Miles?"

"You condemn me, grandfather, without any proof. I haven't the least idea what Lawrence means."

"Do you know one Cuore, an Italian?" asked Larry.

"Never heard of such a person."

"Wait a minute; I will bring the papers, for I am prepared to prove all that I say," said Larry, leaving the room; but he soon returned with a couple of letters in his hand.

"This is all a fiction, Sir Philip," protested Miles.

"We will see whether it is or not," replied Larry. "I have told you about our experience in the French army, and that Phil and I narrowly escaped being shot as spies; but I didn't tell you how we got into the scrape."

My friend detailed our relations with Cuore from the time we first met him in Paris, and showed how he had led us into a doubtful position, and then caused our arrest on the Ticino.

"All that may be, but I had nothing whatever to do with it," said Miles, who had not yet been connected with the affair.

"We found upon the person of the Italian this letter, which contained a draft for money sent to him."

The baronet took the letter, and carefully examined it.

"No signature; but it looks like your writing, Miles."

"It is not my writing, grandfather, and I know nothing about it."

"Then the general opened the mail-bag, in which Cuore had put some letters. One was directed to Miles Grimsby."

"Perhaps it was to my father," said Miles, who now looked pale, and his lip quivered.

"Pshaw, Miles! Your father had not mind enough to write a letter, or to do any business, within the last three months."

"Here is the letter, Sir Philip."

The baronet read it. There could be no doubt that it was addressed to Miles, and the contents fully confirmed all that Larry had declared.

"Then, at Leipsic, I found myself in a balloon car with this same Cuore, who attempted to throw me out, and who, perhaps, would have succeeded if the wound he had received in Italy had not broken out afresh;" and Larry detailed the event with thrilling power.

"That's enough!" exclaimed the baronet. "Miles is as crazy as his father was. I have been too indulgent! I have spoiled the boy. He uses my money to hire an assassin!"

"This is a ridiculous story, Sir Philip, trumped up to prejudice you against me," protested Miles. "There is not a word of truth in it. The story is silly. If the Italian attempted to take his life in the balloon, why didn't he cause his arrest? He doesn't even inquire what became of the man. There isn't a word of truth in the story."

"I would give ten years of my life if I could believe there was not," said the baronet, sadly.

"I am rather sorry I said anything about the matter," added Larry.

"It is best that I should know the truth, bad as it is. I will investigate for myself. No more of my money shall go to pay a bravo."

Miles left the room, no longer able to confront his grandfather's grief and anger.

"What are you going to do, Lawrence, my boy?" asked Sir Philip.

"I am willing to do whatever you may desire, sir."

"Then go to America with your friend. It is better that you should be out of the way for a season. Return in the spring."

We talked till midnight; Sir Philip thought that Larry would be happier in the United States than he would be in England, though he was sorry to part with him; but he hoped to "bring Miles to his senses" before spring.

We remained at Grimsby Hall three days, during which my mother became very much attached to Blanche Fennimore. The poor girl was not happy in her new home. Miles and his mother disliked her on account of her relations to Larry, and her only friend in the house was Sir Philip, who was very kind to her. But she did not feel at home, and she made a confidante of my mother. She desired to return to America, and her wish came to the baronet.

"You will all leave me — will you?" said he to Larry.

"I do not wish to leave you. I am to go by your advice."

"It is better for you to go, and I dare say for Blanche too, for I have to prepare the way for you. Go, and God bless you."

"But Blanche will stay, if you desire it."

"I haven't the heart to ask it. It is no home for a girl like her, while Miles is here. Go, both of you; and it will be different in the spring. Write me every week."

Sir Philip evidently intended to make some change in his household, to reform the evil spirit of Miles. He preferred to do this unobserved by Larry and Blanche. The baronet was very sad when we left him, and Miles kept out of the way. We went to Liverpool, and after a stormy passage, arrived at New York, where we were obliged to remain several days, until Mrs. Collingsby recovered from the effects of the voyage. My mother invited Blanche to go with us to Chicago, but her friends in the city insisted that she should pass the winter with them. Larry, therefore, was not disposed to go away farther with us, though he promised to visit me soon.

We journeyed slowly to Chicago, and when we arrived I confess that my heart bounded with anxiety, as I thought of meeting the Collingsbys there. Joseph had written to them that my mother had acknowledged me as her son, and that he had no doubt of the fact; but I could not see how my grandfather and my uncle Richard would be able to retire from the position they had before taken in regard to me. They were of that sort of people who are determined to be consistent. But I wronged them in my thoughts.

The first person I saw when I entered the house was my father. I was astonished to see him there, and more astonished when my grandfather and my uncle gave me a cordial reception. My father and mother met in perfect reconciliation, and both wept in each other's embrace.

"You were right, Philip," said the elder Mr. Collingsby. "You are my grandson beyond a peradventure. I am satisfied now."

"So am I, sir; and I think I could have convinced you before, if you would have heard me," I replied.

"It would not have done a particle of good to hear you. I should not have believed you if I had heard you. I believed it was all a trick on the part of your father; but he is a new man now, and I am sorry I wronged him."

I could ask for no more, and my happiness was complete. For a week we talked over the past, and lived it over again, both in its joys and its sorrows. But my father's business demanded his return to St. Louis, and my mother and myself went with him. A house had already been provided, and we took immediate possession of it.

For the first time in my life I felt at home. I was in the actual realization of the joys I had anticipated for years. I was under the same roof with my father and my mother, reunited after a separation of fifteen years.

On the evening of the day we entered our new home, my father read a chapter from the Bible, and in his prayer which followed, he uttered the thanksgivings to God that were in all our hearts. Morning and evening he read and prayed, and thus kept himself strong against the temptations that continually beset him.

"I did not believe you would ever reform, Edward," said my mother, one evening after the family devotions.

"I did not believe that I ever should myself; but that good woman, Mrs. Greenough, of whom I have spoken to you, put me on the right track. I had no strength of myself, but God gave it to me when I asked for it. Without my Bible, and without my daily prayer, I am afraid I could not stand a single day. You don't know what power it gives me to feel that God is my ever-present help. I still hanker for whiskey. It has seemed to me, sometimes, that I must drink; and

I know that I should if God did not help me every day and hour that I live."

My mother was deeply impressed by the words of my father. She went to church with him the next Sunday, and attended the evening meetings. His influence soon led her to join him in the Upward and Onward pilgrimage upon which we now all journeyed together. I cannot tell how happy we were, for every hour seemed like a dream of bliss to me. I need hardly say that I did not spend a day in St. Louis without calling upon the Gracewoods. Ella gave me a greeting which assured me that I had still a place in her heart. They came to our house, and my mother thanked them for all they had done for me. The two families were fast friends from the moment they met, and frequent were the visits from one house to the other. Mrs. Greenough was a valued friend of both.

A week before Christmas I had a letter from Larry, promising to spend the holidays with me. He came, and our tongues flew from morning till night.

"I had a letter from Sir Philip the other day," said he. "The old gentleman is taming Miles with a vengeance."

"How taming him?"

"He stopped his money allowance, and keeps a shadow to watch him wherever he goes. But it will do no good."

"If he stops his allowance he cannot employ any such fellow as Cuore to dog you."

"He can raise all the money he wants. The brokers in London will discount his expectations. But never mind him. I have bought a yacht, Phil."

"A yacht!"

"One hundred and twenty tons. She was sold at auction, and I bought her at half her value."

"How do you know she is a good vessel?"

"I got the old sailors to examine her, bored her timbers, and all that sort of thing. She is only two years old, sound as a nut, and took the first prize in half a dozen races. I shall go to England in her in the spring, and you must go with me."

"I can't go."

"What's the reason you can't?" demanded he, excitedly.

"I can't afford to spend any more of my time in that way. My father is not rich; has only his salary of three thousand a year," I replied.

"But your mother's family are rich."

"Undoubtedly; but we have no claims upon them. I must go to work, and earn my own living."

"What are you going to do?"

"I don't know; but I suppose I shall be a clerk."

"How much salary do you expect to get?"

"Eight hundred, or a thousand."

"Good! I appoint you captain of the Blanche, at a salary of one thousand dollars a year."

"Thank you, Larry; you are very kind."

"No, I'm not; none of that."

"I'm certainly very grateful —"

"Dry up! None of your gratitude."

"I should certainly like the position better than anything else I can think of; but I'm afraid my father and mother will not consent to the long absence."

"We will reason with them."

They consented, after a long argument, only to oblige my friend who had saved my life, and because I desired so much to go. Of my experience in the Blanche I have yet to tell, for I sailed in her from New York on the first of April. Larry spent a happy week with me, and I met him again on board of the Blanche about two weeks later. I devoted the rest of the winter to the study of navigation, maritime and naval laws, in order to fit myself for my new position. But whatever else I studied, I could not, in my father's house, forget that the business of this world is not the chief end of existence. I still labored to make my course upward and onward, and endeavored to profit by all the experiences of life, and not least by those of BIVOUAC AND BATTLE.

www.ingramcontent.com/pod-product-compliance
Lightning Source LLC
Chambersburg PA
CBHW030743250426

43672CB00028B/384